2021-2024 RULES

ELVSTRØM EXPLAINS

THE
RACING
RULES

EDITED BY SØREN KRAUSE

ADLARD COLES

LONDON · OXFORD · NEW YORK · NEW DELHI · SYDNEY

ADLARD COLES
Bloomsbury Publishing Plc
50 Bedford Square, London, WC1B 3DP, UK

BLOOMSBURY, ADLARD COLES and the Adlard Coles logo are trademarks of
Bloomsbury Publishing Plc

First published in Great Britain by Creagh-Osborne & Partners Ltd 1965
Second edition 1969, Third edition 1973
Fourth edition 1977, Fifth edition 1981
Sixth edition published by Adlard Coles 1985
Seventh edition 1989
Eighth edition published by Adlard Coles Nautical 1993
Ninth edition 1997, Tenth edition 2001
Eleventh edition 2005, Twelfth edition 2009
Thirteenth edition 2013, Fourteenth edition 2017
This edition published 2020

Bloomsbury Publishing Plc does not have any control over, or responsibility for, any
third-party websites referred to or in this book. All internet addresses given in this
book were correct at the time of going to press. The author and publisher regret
any inconvenience caused if addresses have changed or sites have ceased to
exist, but can accept no responsibility for any such changes

A catalogue record for this book is available from the British Library

Library of Congress Cataloguing-in-Publication data has been applied for

ISBN: PB: 978-1-4729-8059-5; ePub: 978-1-4729-8060-1; ePDF: 978-1-4729-8061-8

2 4 6 8 10 9 7 5 3 1

Typeset in 8.25/10pt Helvetica Light by Margaret Brain
Printed and bound in China by C&C Offset Printing Co., Ltd.

Bloomsbury Publishing Plc makes every effort to ensure that the papers used in the
manufacture of our books are natural, recyclable products made from wood grown in
well-managed forests. Our manufacturing processes conform to the environmental
regulations of the country of origin.

To find out more about our authors and books visit www.bloomsbury.com and
sign up for our newsletters

CONTENTS

*Rules are cross-referenced to the
Explanations and Interpretations by **RED**
numbers in the margins*

FAST FIND DIAGRAM TO PART 2 RULES 'WHEN BOATS MEET'

Black numbers are the Rule numbers
Red numbers refer to the Explanatory Section page numbers

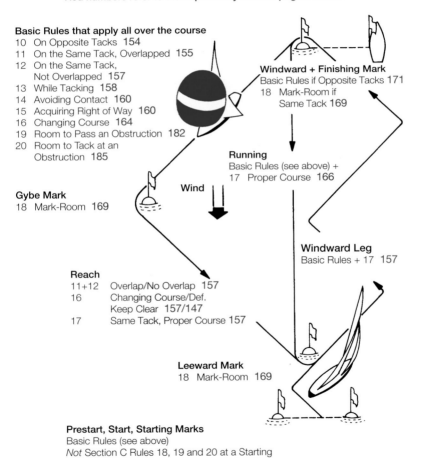

Basic Rules that apply all over the course
10 On Opposite Tacks 154
11 On the Same Tack, Overlapped 155
12 On the Same Tack,
     Not Overlapped 157
13 While Tacking 158
14 Avoiding Contact 160
15 Acquiring Right of Way 160
16 Changing Course 164
19 Room to Pass an Obstruction 182
20 Room to Tack at an
     Obstruction 185

Gybe Mark
18 Mark-Room 169

Windward + Finishing Mark
Basic Rules if Opposite Tacks 171
18 Mark-Room if
     Same Tack 169

Running
Basic Rules (see above) +
17 Proper Course 166

Wind

Windward Leg
Basic Rules + 17 157

Reach
11+12   Overlap/No Overlap 157
16   Changing Course/Def.
          Keep Clear 157/147
17   Same Tack, Proper Course 157

Leeward Mark
18 Mark-Room 169

Prestart, Start, Starting Marks
Basic Rules (see above)
Not Section C Rules 18, 19 and 20 at a Starting
          Mark when approaching to start 170
Not 17! Same Tack, Proper Course before the Starting Signal 157

FOREWORD

Every four years after the Olympic Games, the Racing Rules of Sailing are reviewed. Even if the games are postponed World Sailing have decided to follow the normal four year cycle. Despite constant efforts from the World Sailing Racing Rules Committee to keep the Rules simple and easy to read, they are still quite difficult to understand and may be ambiguous in some situations.

To help to clarify them and ensure uniform interpretation and understanding of their meaning, World Sailing publishes a number of official 'interpretations' or Cases.

Elvstrøm Explains the Racing Rules provides a ready-reference to the Rules, explanatory notes and drawings, and reference to the relevant World Sailing cases in a handy pocket-sized book and now also as an App. Its aim is to help officials and competitors alike to learn the Rules easily, to understand them, and to apply them correctly. It also enables protests and disputes to be resolved fairly.

Elvstrøm Explains the Racing Rules is therefore an invaluable handbook, providing a concise guide to the racing rules for everyone involved in the sport.

Kim Andersen
President World Sailing

INTRODUCTION

The main object of *Elvstrøm explains the Racing Rules* is to provide a handy and easily-read guide for all of us to understand and interpret the rules identically.

The Racing Rules are probably among the most complicated of any sport. They are hard to comprehend even if a great effort is made, when writing the Rules, to use language that is modern and easily read. There is also a constant flow of new interpretations, clarifications and changes to the Rules. Also, the use of the same Rules in match racing and the introduction of 'on the water judging' in fleet races have introduced a more aggressive use of the Rules as a weapon against competitors. The best way to avoid problems is still to sail against others in the same way that you wish to be sailed against. This unwritten rule is the best way of preserving friendships and promoting the desire to participate in sailboat racing.

It is great to win in sailboat racing, but only if the other competitors join in the pleasure.

Paul Elvstrøm

HOW TO GET THE BEST USE OUT OF THIS BOOK

The book is divided into three sections.

1   *The Racing Rules of Sailing* as published by World Sailing.

2   A simple *Explanation* of the various situations that can arise under each rule, supported by bird's-eye-view line drawings.

3   A précis of the cases in *The Case Book* issued by World Sailing, some with bird's-eye-view line drawings.

Following an incident, look up the appropriate rule in the GREY section. This is a facsimile of the Racing Rules. If you don't know the rule number, you might get help from the Fast Find diagram, page 4, for the 'when boats meet' rules, or in the rules contents on page 20 for the rest of the rules.

In the margin opposite the rule will be cross-reference page numbers printed in RED, which refer you to the Explanatory section with RED headbands. From here a new RED number will take you to the relevant Case in the Interpretation Section with RED HATCHED headbands.

The *Explanatory* section is what it says – an explanation of the rule or rules involved, with line drawings to illustrate the points. In the line drawings, the red boat is either wrong, potentially wrong or in the worst position. This way of thinking, always being aware of who is wrong or RED, has proved very useful when racing, especially in match racing, where it is essential to both competitors and umpires to know who is at fault, even before the incident arises.

To support these explanations the Appeal Cases to the Racing Rules are summed up in the *Interpretation* section with the RED HATCHED headbands. These form a Case Law for the Racing Rules of Sailing and are an invaluable cross-reference. It is recommended that both the serious competitor and also the keen student of the rules obtains a copy of the World Sailing Interpretations for the full text, available on www.sailing.org.

I would like to thank World Sailing, especially the members of the Racing Rules Committee and Working Party, for their help and co-operation in producing this book.

Søren Krause
2020

SUMMARY OF CHANGES IN THE 2021–2024 RULES

Most of the changes in the new Rules Book are mostly 'house-keeping' that most sailors will not notice when reading the new rules, correcting minor unintended errors/ambiguities. No major changes to 'The Game' or to the 'Right-of-Way' Rules.

However many editorial changes and changes in rule numbers so care should be taken using references to rule numbers in other documents (including the Case Book) where rule numbers are not yet corrected to 2021–24 rules. See list of new/changed numbers below.

Since 2017 World Sailing has made amendments to cases 78, 116, 132 and published new Cases 141–146.

Following is a summary of the most important changes to the new 2021–2024 rulebook, changes less relevant to most sailors omitted:

Rules deleted from 2017–20 Rules: 5, 6, 7, 14(b), 21, 64.1(a), 75.2, 80, 84, A9, N3.1.

❑ ONLINE RULE DOCUMENTS More documents are available online World Sailing Website; www.sailing.org/documents/

❑ New in INTRODUCTION
Hails can be in other languages if reasonably understood.

World Sailing Codes (old rules 5, 6 and 7 + four more) are now referred to in New rule 6 and no longer by their Regulation Number but simply by their name. All available online.

❑ New in DEFINITIONS.
A boat now *starts* and *finishes* when her **hull** crosses the line. No more discussions on crew or spinnakers and weather they are in normal position. This also apply for the I, Z, U and Black flag start rules.

NOTE spinnaker/equipment are still relevant for determining *overlap*.

New definition *Sail the Course*. The 'string rule' from rule 28 is now a definition. So to complete a race you have to *start, sail the course,* and *finish.* With that there are several editorial changes throughout the rules.

❑ *New rule 5*, RULES GOVERNING ORGANIZING AUTHORITIES AND OFFICIALS is old rule 84.

❏ *New Rule 20.4.* Additional Requirements for Hails. When a hail may not be heard a signal shall be made. The NoR may specify alternative communication.

❏ *New Rule 37 and Flag V:* Search and Rescue Instructions. When flag V is displayed by the Race Committee, instructions are given on the Race Committee channel.

Rule number 2017–2020	Rule number 2021–2024
New Race Signals	Flag V, Orange flag
Online Documents	TBD
New	Introduction, Hails
Introduction, World Sailing Codes	World Sailing Regulations
Introduction, Cases and Calls	Interpretations
New Definition (was part of rule 28.2)	*Sail the Course*
3	4
4	3
5, 6, 7	6
14(b)	43.1(c)
New	20.4
21	43.1(b)
22, 23, 24	21, 22, 23
New	37
New Section A (just a title)	Part 4, Section A, General Requirements
40	40.1, 40.2(a), (b), (c)
New	43.1(a), (b), (c); 43.2
55	47
47, 47.1, 47.2	48, 48.1, 48.2
New Section B (just a title)	Part 4, Section B, Equibment-Related Rules
43, 43.1(a) and (b), 43.2	50, 50.1(a) and (b), 50.2
New	50.1(c)
50, 50.1, 50.2, 50.3(a), (b), (c), 50.4	55, 55.1, 55.2, 55.3(a), (b), (c), (d), 55.4
48, 48.1, 48.2	56, 56.1, 56.2
New	60.1(c)
New	62.2(a)
63.6	63.6(a), (b), (c), (d)
New	63.9
New	64.1(a), (b), (c)
64.1, 64.2, 64.3, 64.4	64.2, 64.3, 64.4, 64.5
New	64.6

New	65.3
65.3	65.4
66	66.1, 66.2, 66.3
75.1	75
75.2	Deleted
80	6.1
81	80
84	5
New	90.3(d), (e)
A4.1	A4
A4.2	A5.1
A5	A5.3
A9	A5.2
A10, A11	A9, A10

Appendices

Appendix B – Windsurfing Rules	Substantially revised
Appendix J – NOR and SI	Substantially revised
Appendix K – Notice of Race Guide	*Deleted from RRS. Will be online as fillable template*
Appendix L – Sailing instructions Guide	*Deleted from RRS. Will be online as fillable template*
Protest Form	*Deleted from RRS*
Replaced by	
Hearing Request Form	*Will be online as a fillable template.*
Hearing Decision Form	*Will be online as a fillable template*

Rule Title Changes for 2021–2024
(Covers Parts 1-7 and Appendix A)
(Changes from the 2017–2020 edition shown in red)

New Definition: *Sail the Course*

1	SAFETY
1.1	Helping Those in Danger
1.2	Life-Saving Equipment and Personal Flotation Devices
2	FAIR SAILING
3	DECISION TO RACE
4	ACCEPTANCE OF THE RULES
5	RULES GOVERNING ORGANIZING AUTHORITIES AND OFFICIALS
6	WORLD SAILING REGULATIONS
10	ON OPPOSITE TACKS
11	ON THE SAME TACK, OVERLAPPED
12	ON THE SAME TACK, NOT OVERLAPPED
13	WHILE TACKING
14	AVOIDING CONTACT
15	ACQUIRING RIGHT OF WAY
16	CHANGING COURSE
17	ON THE SAME TACK; PROPER COURSE
18	MARK-ROOM
18.1	When Rule 18 Applies
18.2	Giving Mark-Room
18.3	Passing Head to Wind in the Zone
18.4	Gybing
19	ROOM TO PASS AN OBSTRUCTION
19.1	When Rule 19 Applies
19.2	Giving Room at an Obstruction
20	ROOM TO TACK AT AN OBSTRUCTION

New Section Titles in Part 4:

BRIEF NOTES OF GUIDANCE FOR MAKING A PROTEST/REQUEST A HEARING

1 Following an incident you must quickly reach a decision – are you in the wrong? In which case you must either accept a penalty or retire. Or are you the aggrieved boat? In which case you must protest to tell the other boat you think she broke a rule (Rule 60.1). Of course, if the other boat accepts a penalty or retires as a result of this infringement, filing the protest will not be necessary. But do not come ashore and grumble about the foul and that you failed to protest.

2 Be sure in your mind that having decided to protest you have a) tried to inform the other boat (a hail is mandatory if the incident is in the racing area and you are within hailing distance) and b) displayed a protest flag at the first reasonable opportunity (Rule 61.1a) unless your hull is less than 6 meters (Rule 61.1a2).

3 Immediately try to identify any possible witnesses from nearby boats.

4 After the incident quickly go over the events that led up to the infringement so as to be quite clear about the manner in which it happened. If it is possible, scribble some notes to remind you later about the exact details. Discuss it briefly with your crew if you think it will help. However you should be careful not to spend too much time on the incident while still racing as this could impair your performance.

5 Be sure that the Race Committee acknowledges your intention to protest as you finish if required by the Sailing Instructions or Class Rules.

6 Once ashore you have several tasks to complete before lodging the protest:
(a) Check the latest time for lodging a Protest (Rule 61.3). It is usually two hours after the last boat finishing but can be varied by the Sailing Instructions. The Protest Time is usually posted on the Official Notice Board; check the Sailing Instructions.
(b) Again be sure that you have tried to inform the protested boat (Rule 61.1a).
(c) Contact your possible witnesses and ask them to attend the hearing if you feel they will support your case. Make sure that

your witnesses will be positive to your case in their testimony. Simply padding out your case with a large number of witnesses who have little to add to the facts will do nothing but keep everybody in the Protest Room longer than they wish and may alienate the Protest Committee. Do not rehearse your witness. It is usually very obvious that he or she has been set up in your favour and this may legislate against you.

(d) Think the incident through again. By now, you should be in a position to set out the incident as you saw it and the rest of the contents, on the Hearing Request Form (Rule 61.2). A fillable form is available on the World Sailing webside or the Race Office should be able to supply/print one. If not, any sheet of paper will do, provided it is not tatty or soggy; the Protest Committee has to read it. Do not put too much detail on the Hearing Form. You can find details of what is required in Rule 61.2. A short description of the incident is all that is necessary. Add details of where and when it took place to make sure everybody knows exactly which incident you are referring to. There may have been several. If possible, add a note of which Rules you think have been infringed. A clear diagram is usually very helpful. (Use the 'ruler' with the models in the cover wallet and see example of a drawing). A god diagram starts building the picture of the situation that you want in the mind of the protest committee members, so you gain an advantage even before the hearing has started.

(e) One final point to consider, before lodging your protest: if the onus is on you to prove your case, and there is no positive witness in your favour and the evidence is poor, think very carefully before lodging the protest. You have to have a very good case; otherwise it is a lost cause. Such circumstances are when the overlap situation changes just before entering the zone. When an outside boat breaks an overlap or a boat clear astern establishes an inside overlap just before the boats enter the zone. (Rule 18.2(d)).

7 Now lodge the protest. No action can be taken by the Protest Committee to hear your protest unless you lodge it within the required time limit. Remember, once you have lodged a protest it must be heard unless the Protest Committee approves your request to have it withdrawn. (Rule 63.1).

8 Make sure you know where and when your protest is to be heard. The Sailing Instructions should detail where the notice will be posted.

9 During the hearing, which should follow the procedure set out in Appendix M, treat the Protest Committee with respect. They will almost certainly be sailors like you, doing their best for everybody concerned. Do not be rude or lose your temper. It will do nothing to further your case.

10 In establishing your case it is often helpful to work back from the incident. The facts as you see them will come out during the hearing. The following table of the rate of advance of a boat may be a helpful guideline in establishing distances.

1kt = 0.51 m/sec
2kt = 1.03 m/sec
3kt = 1.54 m/sec
4kt = 2.11 m/sec
5kt = 2.57 m/sec
6kt = 3.09 m/sec
7kt = 3.60 m/sec
8kt = 4.12 m/sec
9kt = 4.63 m/sec
10kt= 5.14 m/sec

11 Remember there is no substitute for care in the preparation of your case.

12 A point for Protest Committees – it is very helpful to the competitor if you give some explanation of the background when you announce your decision. Not only will the competitor learn from that, but it will go a long way towards maintaining the good spirit of the event.

THE RACING RULES OF SAILING FOR 2021–2024

CONTENTS

ONLINE RULES DOCUMENTS

World Sailing has established a single internet address at which readers will find links to all the documents available on the World Sailing website that are mentioned in this book. Those documents are listed below. Links to other rules documents will also be provided at that address.

The address is: sailing.org/racingrules/documents.

Document	Mentioned in
Guidelines for discretionary penalties	Introduction
Changes made to these rules after 1 January 2021	Introdution
World Sailing Regulations	Introduction
The Case Book	Introduction
The Call Books for various disciplines	Introduction
World Sailing Regulations with the status of a *rule*	Definition Rule (b)
Interpretations of Rule 42, Propulsion	Rule 42
World Sailing Offshore Special Regulations	Rule 49.2
Appendix TS, Traffic Separation Schemes	Rule 56.2
Hearing Request and Hearing Decision Forms	Part 5 Preamble
Rules for other windsurfing competition formats	Appendix B Preamble
Standard Notice of Race for Match Racing	Appendix C Preamble
Standard Sailing Instructions for Match Racing	Appendix C Preamble
Match Racing Rules for Blind Competitors	Appendix C Preamble
Test Rules for Umpired Radio Sailing	Appendix E Preamble
Rules for other kiteboarding competition formats	Appendix F Preamble
Up-to-date table of national sail letters	Rule G
Notice of Race Guide	Appendix K Notice
Sailing Instructions Guide	Appendix L Notice
Guidance on conflicts of interest	Appendix M2.3
Guidance on misconduct	Appendix M5.8
World Sailing Judges Manual	Appendix T Preamble

INTRODUCTION

The Racing Rules of Sailing includes two main sections. The first, Parts 1–7, contains rules that affect all competitors. The second, the appendices, provides details of rules, rules that apply to particular kinds of racing, and rules that affect only a small number of competitors or officials.

Terminology

A term used in the sense stated in the Definitions is printed in italics or, in preambles, in bold italics (for example, *racing* and ***racing***).

Each of the terms in the table below is used in *The Racing Rules of Sailing* with the meaning given.

Term	Meaning
Boat	A sailboat and the crew on board.
Competitor	A person who races or intends to race in the event.
National authority	A World Sailing member national authority.
Race committee	The race committee appointed under rule 89.2(c) and any other person or committee performing a race committee function.
Racing rule	A rule in *The Racing Rules of Sailing*.
Technical committee	The technical committee appointed under rule 89.2(c) and any other person or committee performing a technical committee function.
Vessel	Any boat or ship.

Other words and terms are used in the sense ordinarily understood in nautical or general use.

Hails

A language other than English may be used for a hail required by the *rules* provided that it is reasonable for it to be understood by all boats affected. However, a hail in English is always acceptable.

Notation

The notation '[DP]' in a *rule* means that the penalty for a breach of the *rule* may, at the discretion of the protest committee, be less than disqualification. Guidelines for discretionary penalties are available on the World Sailing website.

Revision

The racing rules are revised and published every four years by World Sailing, the international authority for the sport. This edition becomes effective on 1 January 2021 except that for an event beginning in 2020 the date may be postponed by the notice of race or sailing instructions. Marginal markings indicate important changes to Parts 1–7 and the Definitions in the 2017–2020 edition. No changes are contemplated before 2025, but any changes determined to be urgent before then will be announced through national authorities and posted on the World Sailing website.

Appendices

When the rules of an appendix apply, they take precedence over any conflicting rules in Parts 1–7 and the Definitions. Each appendix is identified by a letter. A reference to a rule in an appendix will contain the letter and the rule number (for example, 'rule A1'). The letters I, O and Q are not used to designate appendices in this book.

World Sailing Regulations

The Regulations are referred to in the definition *Rule* and in rule 6, but they are not included in this book because they can be changed at any time. The most recent versions of the Regulations are published on the World Sailing website; new versions will be announced through national authorities.

Interpretations

World Sailing publishes the following authoritative interpretations of the racing rules:

- *The Case Book – Interpretations of the Racing Rules,*
- *The Call Books*, for various disciplines,
- Interpretations of Rule 42, Propulsion, and
- Interpretations of the Regulations, for those Regulations that are *rules*.

These publications are available on the World Sailing website. Other interpretations of the racing rules are not authoritative unless approved by World Sailing in accordance with Regulation 28.4.

DEFINITIONS

A term used as stated below is shown in italic type or, in preambles, in bold italic type. The meaning of several other terms is given in Terminology in the Introduction.

Abandon A race that a race committee or protest committee *abandons* is void but may be resailed.

146✸ **Clear Astern** and **Clear Ahead; Overlap** One boat is *clear astern* of another when her hull and equipment in normal position are behind a line abeam from the aftermost point of the other boat's hull and equipment in normal position. The other boat is *clear ahead.* They *overlap* when neither is *clear astern.* However, they also *overlap* when

146✸ a boat between them *overlaps* both. These terms always apply to boats on the same *tack.* They apply to boats on opposite *tacks* only when rule 18 applies between them or when both boats are sailing more than ninety degrees from the true wind.

Conflict of Interest A person has a *conflict of interest* if he
(a) may gain or lose as a result of a decision to which he contributes,
(b) may reasonably appear to have a personal or financial interest which could affect his ability to be impartial, or
(c) has a close personal interest in a decision.

179/ **Fetching** A boat is *fetching* a *mark* when she is in a position to pass to
189✸ windward of it and leave it on the required side without changing *tack.*

148✸ **Finish** A boat *finishes* when, after *starting*, any part of her hull crosses the finishing line from the course side. However, she has not *finished* if after crossing the finishing line she
(a) takes a penalty under rule 44.2,
(b) corrects an error in *sailing the course* made at the line, or
(c) continues to *sail the course.*

149✸ **Keep Clear** A boat *keeps clear* of a right-of-way boat
(a) if the right-of-way boat can sail her course with no need to take avoiding action and,
(b) when the boats are *overlapped*, if the right-of-way boat can also change course in both directions without immediately making contact.

149✸ **Leeward** and **Windward** A boat's *leeward* side is the side that is or, when she is head to wind, was away from the wind. However, when sailing by the lee or directly downwind, her *leeward* side is the side on which her mainsail lies. The other side is her *windward* side. When two boats on the same *tack overlap*, the one on the *leeward* side of the other is the *leeward* boat. The other is the *windward* boat.

197✸ **Mark** An object the sailing instructions require a boat to leave on a specified side, a race committee vessel surrounded by navigable water from which the starting or finishing line extends, and an object

Definitions

intentionally attached to the object or vessel. However, an anchor line is not part of the *mark*.

Mark-Room *Room* for a boat to leave a *mark* on the required side. Also,
(a) *room* to sail to the *mark* when her *proper course* is to sail close to it, and
(b) *room* to round or pass the *mark* as necessary to *sail the course* without touching the *mark*.

However, *mark-room* for a boat does not include *room* to tack unless she is *overlapped* inside and to *windward* of the boat required to give *mark-room* and she would be *fetching* the *mark* after her tack.

Obstruction An object that a boat could not pass without changing course substantially, if she were sailing directly towards it and one of her hull lengths from it. An object that can be safely passed on only one side and an object, area or line so designated by the sailing instructions are also *obstructions*. However, a boat *racing* is not an *obstruction* to other boats unless they are required to *keep clear* of her or, if rule 22 applies, avoid her. A vessel under way, including a boat *racing*, is never a continuing *obstruction*.

Overlap See **Clear Astern** and **Clear Ahead**; **Overlap**.

Party A *party* to a hearing is
(a) for a protest hearing: a protestor, a protestee;
(b) for a redress hearing: a boat requesting redress or for which redress is requested; a boat for which a hearing is called to consider redress under rule 60.3(b); a race committee acting under rule 60.2(b); a technical committee acting under rule 60.4(b);
(c) for a redress hearing under rule 62.1(a): the body alleged to have made an improper action or omission;
(d) a person against whom an allegation of a breach of rule 69.1(a) is made; a person presenting an allegation under rule 69.2(e)(1);
(e) a *support person* subject to a hearing under rule 60.3(d) or 69; any boat that person supports; a person appointed to present an allegation under rule 60.3(d).

However, the protest committee is never a *party*.

Postpone A *postponed* race is delayed before its scheduled start but may be started or *abandoned* later.

Proper Course A course a boat would choose in order to *sail* the course and *finish* as soon as possible in the absence of the other boats referred to in the rule using the term. A boat has no *proper course* before her starting signal.

Protest An allegation made under rule 61.2 by a boat, a race committee, a technical committee or a protest committee that a boat has broken a *rule*.

Racing A boat is *racing* from her preparatory signal until she *finishes* and clears the finishing line and *marks* or retires, or until the race committee signals a general recall, *postponement* or *abandonment*.

page
*198
*172
*150
*150
*157
*148
*198

page

Room The space a boat needs in the existing conditions, including space to comply with her obligations under the rules of Part 2 and rule 31, while manoeuvring promptly in a seamanlike way.

151✱

151✱ **Rule**

(a) The rules in this book, including the Definitions, Race Signals, Introduction, preambles and the rules of relevant appendices, but not titles;

(b) World Sailing Regulations that have been designated by World Sailing as having the status of a *rule* and are published on the World Sailing website;

(c) the prescriptions of the national authority, unless they are changed by the notice of race or sailing instructions in compliance with the national authority's prescription, if any, to rule 88.2;

(d) the class rules (for a boat racing under a handicap or rating system, the rules of that system are 'class rules');

(e) the notice of race;

(f) the sailing instructions; and

(g) any other documents that govern the event.

216✱ **Sail the Course** A boat *sails the course* provided that a string representing her track from the time she begins to approach the starting line from its pre-start side to *start* until she *finishes*, when drawn taut,

(a) passes each *mark* of the course for the race on the required side and in the correct order,

(b) touches each *mark* designated in the sailing instructions to be a rounding *mark*, and

(c) passes between the *marks* of a gate from the direction of the course from the previous *mark*.

151✱ **Start** A boat *starts* when, her hull having been entirely on the pre-start side of the starting line at or after her starting signal, and having complied with rule 30.1 if it applies, any part of her hull crosses the starting line from the pre-start side to the course side.

Support Person Any person who

(a) provides, or may provide, physical or advisory support to a competitor, including any coach, trainer, manager, team staff, medic, paramedic or any other person working with, treating or assisting a competitor in or preparing for the competition, or

(b) is the parent or guardian of a competitor.

149✱ **Tack, Starboard or Port** A boat is on the *tack, starboard* or *port*, corresponding to her *windward* side.

Windward See **Leeward** and **Windward**.

Zone The area around a *mark* within a distance of three hull lengths of the boat nearer to it. A boat is in the *zone* when any part of her hull is in the *zone*.

BASIC PRINCIPLES

Sportsmanship and the Rules

Competitors in the sport of sailing are governed by a body of *rules* that they are expected to follow and enforce. A fundamental principle of sportsmanship is that when a boat breaks a *rule* and is not exonerated she will promptly take an appropriate penalty or action, which may be to retire.

Environmental Responsibility

Participants are encouraged to minimize any adverse environmental impact of the sport of sailing.

PART 1 – FUNDAMENTAL RULES

1   SAFETY

1.1   Helping Those in Danger

※152

A boat, competitor or *support person* shall give all possible help to any person or vessel in danger.

1.2   Life-Saving Equipment and Personal Flotation Devices

※152

A boat shall carry adequate life-saving equipment for all persons on board, including one item ready for immediate use, unless her class rules make some other provision. Each competitor is individually responsible for wearing a personal flotation device adequate for the conditions.

2   FAIR SAILING

※152

A boat and her owner shall compete in compliance with recognized principles of sportsmanship and fair play. A boat may be penalized under this rule only if it is clearly established that these principles have been violated. The penalty shall be disqualification that is not excludable.

3   DECISION TO RACE

※152

The responsibility for a boat's decision to participate in a race or to continue *racing* is hers alone.

4   ACCEPTANCE OF THE RULES

※152

4.1   (a) By participating or intending to participate in an event conducted under the *rules*, each competitor and boat owner agrees to accept the *rules*.

(b) A *support person* by providing support, or a parent or guardian by permitting their child to enter an event, agrees to accept the *rules*.

4.2 Each competitor and boat owner agrees, on behalf of their *support persons*, that such *support persons* are bound by the *rules*.

4.3 Acceptance of the *rules* includes agreement
(a) to be governed by the *rules*;
(b) to accept the penalties imposed and other action taken under the *rules*, subject to the appeal and review procedures provided in them, as the final determination of any matter arising under the *rules*;
(c) with respect to any such determination, not to resort to any court of law or tribunal not provided for in the *rules*; and
(d) by each competitor and boat owner to ensure that their *support persons* are aware of the *rules*.

4.4 The person in charge of each boat shall ensure that all competitors in the crew and the boat's owner are aware of their responsibilities under this rule.

4.5 This rule may be changed by a prescription of the national authority of the venue.

203✳ **5** **RULES GOVERNING ORGANIZING AUTHORITIES AND OFFICIALS**
The organizing authority, race committee, technical committee, protest committee and other race officials shall be governed by the *rules* in the conduct and judging of the event.

6 **WORLD SAILING REGULATIONS**

153✳ **6.1** Each competitor, boat owner and *support person* shall comply with the World Sailing Regulations that have been designated by World Sailing as having the status of a *rule*. These regulations as of 30 June 2020 are the World Sailing:
• Advertising Code
• Anti-Doping Code
• Betting and Anti-Corruption Code
• Disciplinary Code
• Eligibility Code
• Sailor Categorization Code

6.2 Rule 63.1 does not apply unless *protests* are permitted in the Regulation alleged to have been broken.

PART 2 – WHEN BOATS MEET

*The rules of Part 2 apply between boats that are sailing in or near the racing area and intend to **race**, are **racing**, or have been **racing**. However, a boat not **racing** shall not be penalized for breaking one of these rules, except rule 14 when the incident resulted in injury or serious damage, or rule 23.1.*

❉*153*

When a boat sailing under these rules meets a vessel that is not, she shall comply with the International Regulations for Preventing Collisions at Sea (IRPCAS) or government right-of-way rules. If the notice of race so states, the rules of Part 2 are replaced by the right-of- way rules of the IRPCAS or by government right-of-way rules.

Section A – Right of Way
*A boat has right of way over another boat when the other boat is required to **keep clear** of her. However, some rules in Sections B, C and D limit the actions of a right-of-way boat.*

10   ON OPPOSITE TACKS
When boats are on opposite *tacks*, a *port-tack* boat shall *keep clear* of a *starboard-tack* boat.

❉*154*

11   ON THE SAME TACK, OVERLAPPED
When boats are on the same *tack* and *overlapped*, a *windward* boat shall *keep clear* of a *leeward* boat.

❉*155*

12   ON THE SAME TACK, NOT OVERLAPPED
When boats are on the same *tack* and not *overlapped*, a boat *clear astern* shall *keep clear* of a boat *clear ahead*.

❉*157*

13   WHILE TACKING
After a boat passes head to wind, she shall *keep clear* of other boats until she is on a close-hauled course. During that time rules 10, 11 and 12 do not apply. If two boats are subject to this rule at the same time, the one on the other's port side or the one astern shall *keep clear*.

❉*158*

Section B – General Limitations

160✻ 14 **AVOIDING CONTACT**

159✻ A boat shall avoid contact with another boat if reasonably possible. However, a right-of-way boat, or one sailing within the *room* or *mark-room* to which she is entitled, need not act to avoid contact until it is clear that the other boat is not *keeping clear* or giving *room* or *mark-room*.

160✻ 15 **ACQUIRING RIGHT OF WAY**

When a boat acquires right of way, she shall initially give the other boat *room* to *keep clear*, unless she acquires right of way because of the other boat's actions.

164✻ 16 **CHANGING COURSE**

16.1 When a right-of-way boat changes course, she shall give the other boat *room* to *keep clear.*

16.2 In addition, on a beat to windward when a *port-tack* boat is *keeping clear* by sailing to pass to leeward of a *starboard-tack* boat, the *starboard-tack* boat shall not bear away if as a result the *port-tack* boat must change course immediately to continue *keeping clear.*

166✻ 17 **ON THE SAME TACK; PROPER COURSE**

If a boat *clear astern* becomes *overlapped* within two of her hull lengths to *leeward* of a boat on the same *tack*, she shall not sail above her *proper course* while they remain on the same *tack* and *overlapped* within that distance, unless in doing so she promptly sails astern of the other boat. This rule does not apply if the *overlap* begins while the *windward* boat is required by rule 13 to *keep clear*.

170✻ ## Section C – At Marks and Obstructions

Section C rules do not apply at a starting **mark** *surrounded by navigable water or at its anchor line from the time boats are approaching them to* **start** *until they have passed them.*

18 MARK-ROOM

170✻ **18.1 When Rule 18 Applies**

Rule 18 applies between boats when they are required to leave a *mark* on the same side and at least one of them is in the *zone*. However, it does not apply

171✻ (a) between boats on opposite *tacks* on a beat to windward,

(b) between boats on opposite *tacks* when the *proper course* at the *mark* for one but not both of them is to tack,

(c) between a boat approaching a *mark* and one leaving it, or

(d) if the *mark* is a continuing *obstruction*, in which case rule 19 applies.

Rule 18 no longer applies between boats when *mark-room* has been given.

18.2 Giving Mark-Room

(a) When boats are *overlapped* the outside boat shall give the inside boat *mark-room*, unless rule 18.2(b) applies.   * 172

(b) If boats are *overlapped* when the first of them reaches the *zone*, the outside boat at that moment shall thereafter give the inside boat *mark-room*. If a boat is *clear ahead* when she reaches the *zone*, the boat *clear astern* at that moment shall thereafter give her *mark-room*.   * 174   * 173/ 176

(c) When a boat is required to give *mark-room* by rule 18.2(b),

  (1) she shall continue to do so even if later an *overlap* is broken or a new *overlap* begins;   * 173

  (2) if she becomes *overlapped* inside the boat entitled to *mark-room*, she shall also give that boat *room* to sail her *proper course* while they remain *overlapped*.   * 173

(d) Rules 18.2(b) and (c) cease to apply if the boat entitled to *mark-room* passes head to wind or leaves the *zone*.   * 177

(e) If there is reasonable doubt that a boat obtained or broke an *overlap* in time, it shall be presumed that she did not.   * 178

(f) If a boat obtained an inside *overlap* from *clear astern* or by tacking to *windward* of the other boat and, from the time the *overlap* began, the outside boat has been unable to give *mark-room*, she is not required to give it.   * 175

18.3 Passing Head to Wind in the Zone

If a boat in the *zone* of a *mark* to be left to port passes head to wind from *port* to *starboard tack* and is then *fetching* the *mark*, she shall not cause a boat that has been on *starboard tack* since entering the *zone* to sail above close-hauled to avoid contact and she shall give *mark-room* if that boat becomes *overlapped* inside her. When this rule applies between boats, rule 18.2 does not apply between them.   * 179

18.4 Gybing

When an inside *overlapped* right-of-way boat must gybe at a *mark* to sail her *proper course*, until she gybes she shall sail no farther from the *mark* than needed to sail that course. Rule 18.4 does not apply at a gate *mark*.   * 181

page

19   ROOM TO PASS AN OBSTRUCTION

182✸   **19.1 When Rule 19 Applies**

Rule 19 applies between two boats at an *obstruction* except

(a) when the *obstruction* is a *mark* the boats are required to leave on the same side, or

(b) when rule 18 applies between the boats and the *obstruction* is another boat *overlapped* with each of them.

However, at a continuing *obstruction*, rule 19 always applies and rule 18 does not.

182✸   **19.2 Giving Room at an Obstruction**

(a) A right-of-way boat may choose to pass an *obstruction* on either side.

183✸   (b) When boats are *overlapped*, the outside boat shall give the inside boat *room* between her and the *obstruction*, unless she has been unable to do so from the time the *overlap* began.

184✸   (c) While boats are passing a continuing *obstruction*, if a boat that was *clear astern* and required to *keep clear* becomes *overlapped* between the other boat and the *obstruction* and, at the moment the *overlap* begins, there is not *room* for her to pass between them,

(1) she is not entitled to *room* under rule 19.2(b), and

(2) while the boats remain *overlapped*, she shall keep *clear* and rules 10 and 11 do not apply.

185✸   **20   ROOM TO TACK AT AN OBSTRUCTION**

20.1 Hailing

A boat may hail for *room* to tack and avoid a boat on the same *tack*. However, she shall not hail unless

(a) she is approaching an *obstruction* and will soon need to make a substantial course change to avoid it safely, and

(b) she is sailing close-hauled or above.

189✸   In addition, she shall not hail if the obstruction is a *mark* and a boat that is *fetching* it would be required to change course as a result of the hail.

20.2 Responding

185✸   (a) After a boat hails, she shall give a hailed boat time to respond.

(b) A hailed boat shall respond even if the hail breaks rule 20.1.

185✸   (c) A hailed boat shall respond either by tacking as soon as possible, or by immediately replying 'You tack' and then giving the hailing boat *room* to tack and avoid her.

(d) When a hailed boat responds, the hailing boat shall tack as soon as possible.

(e) From the time a boat hails until she has tacked and avoided a hailed boat, rule 18.2 does not apply between them.

20.3 Passing On a Hail to an Additional Boat ✹*187*

When a boat has been hailed for *room* to tack and she intends to respond by tacking, she may hail another boat on the same *tack* for *room* to tack and avoid her. She may hail even if her hail does not meet the conditions of rule 20.1. Rule 20.2 applies between her and a boat she hails.

20.4 Additional Requirements for Hails

(a) When conditions are such that a hail may not be heard, the boat shall also make a signal that clearly indicates her need for *room* to tack or her response.

(b) The notice of race may specify an alternative communication for a boat to indicate her need for *room* to tack or her response, and require boats to use it.

Section D – Other Rules

When rule 21 or 22 applies between two boats, Section A rules do not.

21 STARTING ERRORS; TAKING PENALTIES; BACKING A SAIL

21.1 A boat sailing towards the pre-start side of the starting line or ✹*190* one of its extensions after her starting signal to *start* or to comply with rule 30.1 shall *keep clear* of a boat not doing so until her hull is completely on the pre-start side.

21.2 A boat taking a penalty shall *keep clear* of one that is not. ✹*193*

21.3 A boat moving astern, or sideways to windward, through the ✹*192* water by backing a sail shall *keep clear* of one that is not.

22 CAPSIZED, ANCHORED OR AGROUND; RESCUING ✹*193*

If possible, a boat shall avoid a boat that is capsized or has not regained control after capsizing, is anchored or aground, or is trying to help a person or vessel in danger. A boat is capsized when her masthead is in the water.

23 INTERFERING WITH ANOTHER BOAT

23.1 If reasonably possible, a boat not *racing* shall not interfere with a boat that is *racing*.

23.2 If reasonably possible, a boat shall not interfere with a boat that is taking a penalty, sailing on another leg or subject to rule 21.1. However, after the starting signal this rule does not apply when the boat is sailing her *proper course*.

PART 3 – CONDUCT OF A RACE

195✳ **25   NOTICE OF RACE, SAILING INSTRUCTIONS AND SIGNALS**

25.1 The notice of race shall be made available to each boat that enters an event before she enters. The sailing instructions shall be made available to each boat before a race begins.

25.2 The meanings of the visual and sound signals stated in Race Signals shall not be changed except under rule 86.1(b). The meanings of any other signals that may be used shall be stated in the notice of race or sailing instructions.

25.3 When the race committee is required to display a flag as a visual signal, it may use a flag or other object of a similar appearance.

195✳ **26   STARTING RACES**
Races shall be started by using the following signals. Times shall be taken from the visual signals; the absence of a sound signal shall be disregarded.

Minutes before starting signal	Visual signal	Sound signal	Means
5*	Class flag	One	Warning signal
4	P, I, Z, Z with I, U or black flag	One	Preparatory signal
1	Preparatory flag removed	One long	One minute
0	Class flag removed	One	Starting signal

*or as stated in the notice of race or sailing instructions

The warning signal for each succeeding class shall be made with or after the starting signal of the preceding class.

page

27 OTHER RACE COMMITTEE ACTIONS BEFORE THE STARTING SIGNAL

27.1 No later than the warning signal, the race committee shall signal or otherwise designate the course to be sailed if the sailing instructions have not stated the course, and it may replace one course signal with another and signal that wearing personal flotation devices is required (display flag Y with one sound).

27.2 No later than the preparatory signal, the race committee may move a starting *mark*.

27.3 Before the starting signal, the race committee may for any reason *postpone* (display flag AP, AP over H, or AP over A, with two sounds) or *abandon* the race (display flag N over H, or N over A, with three sounds).

28 SAILING THE RACE

✸ *195/* 196

28.1 A boat shall *start*, *sail the course* and then *finish*. While doing so, she may leave on either side a *mark* that does not begin, bound or end the leg she is sailing. After *finishing* she need not cross the finishing line completely.

✸ *197*

28.2 A boat may correct any errors in *sailing the course*, provided she has not crossed the finishing line to *finish*.

✸ *196*

29 RECALLS

29.1 Individual Recall

✸ *198*

When at a boat's starting signal any part of her hull is on the course side of the starting line or she must comply with rule 30.1, the race committee shall promptly display flag X with one sound. The flag shall be displayed until the hull of each such boat has been completely on the pre-start side of the starting line or one of its extensions, and until all such boats have complied with rule 30.1 if it applies, but no later than four minutes after the starting signal or one minute before any later starting signal, whichever is earlier. If rule 29.2, 30.3 or 30.4 applies this rule does not.

29.2 General Recall

When at the starting signal the race committee is unable to identify boats that are on the course side of the starting line or to which rule 30 applies, or there has been an error in the starting procedure, the race committee may signal a general recall (display the First Substitute with two sounds). The warning signal for a new start for the recalled class shall be made one minute after the First Substitute is removed (one sound), and the starts for any succeeding classes shall follow the new start.

195 ✳

30   STARTING PENALTIES

30.1   I Flag Rule

If flag I has been displayed, and any part of a boat's hull is on the course side of the starting line or one of its extensions during the last minute before her starting signal, she shall sail across an extension so that her hull is completely on the pre-start side before she *starts*.

30.2   Z Flag Rule

If flag Z has been displayed, no part of a boat's hull shall be in the triangle formed by the ends of the starting line and the first *mark* during the last minute before her starting signal. If a boat breaks this rule and is identified, she shall receive, without a hearing, a 20% Scoring Penalty calculated as stated in rule 44.3(c). She shall be penalized even if the race is restarted or resailed, but not if it is *postponed* or *abandoned* before the starting signal. If she is similarly identified during a subsequent attempt to start the same race, she shall receive an additional 20% Scoring Penalty.

30.3   U Flag Rule

If flag U has been displayed, no part of a boat's hull shall be in the triangle formed by the ends of the starting line and the first *mark* during the last minute before her starting signal. If a boat breaks this rule and is identified, she shall be disqualified without a hearing, but not if the race is restarted or resailed.

30.4   Black Flag Rule

If a black flag has been displayed, no part of a boat's hull shall be in the triangle formed by the ends of the starting line and the first *mark* during the last minute before her starting signal. If a boat breaks this rule and is identified, she shall be disqualified without a hearing, even if the race is restarted or resailed, but not if it is *postponed* or *abandoned* before the starting signal. If a general recall is signalled or the race is *abandoned* after the starting signal, the race committee shall display her sail number before the next warning signal for that race, and if the race is restarted or resailed she shall not sail in it. If she does so, her disqualification shall not be excluded in calculating her series score.

198 ✳

198/
199 ✳

199 ✳

31   TOUCHING A MARK

While *racing*, a boat shall not touch a starting *mark* before *starting*, a *mark* that begins, bounds or ends the leg of the course on which she is sailing, or a finishing *mark* after *finishing*.

32 SHORTENING OR ABANDONING AFTER THE START

32.1 After the starting signal, the race committee may shorten the course (display flag S with two sounds) or *abandon* the race (display flag N, N over H, or N over A, with three sounds),

(a) because of foul weather,

(b) because of insufficient wind making it unlikely that any boat will *finish* within the race time limit,

(c) because a *mark* is missing or out of position, or

(d) for any other reason directly affecting the safety or fairness of the competition.

In addition, the race committee may shorten the course so that other scheduled races can be sailed, or *abandon* the race because of an error in the starting procedure. However, after one boat has *started*, *sailed the course* and *finished* within the race time limit, if any, the race committee shall not *abandon* the race without considering the consequences for all boats in the race or series.

✹*200*

32.2 If the race committee signals a shortened course (displays flag S with two sounds), the finishing line shall be,

(a) at a rounding *mark*, between the *mark* and a staff displaying flag S;

(b) a line the course requires boats to cross; or

(c) at a gate, between the gate marks.

The shortened course shall be signalled before the first boat crosses the finishing line.

33 CHANGING THE NEXT LEG OF THE COURSE

While boats are *racing*, the race committee may change a leg of the course that begins at a rounding *mark* or at a gate by changing the position of the next *mark* (or the finishing line) and signalling all boats before they begin the leg. The next *mark* need not be in position at that time.

(a) If the direction of the leg will be changed, the signal shall be the display of flag C with repetitive sounds and one or both of

(1) the new compass bearing,

(2) a green triangle for a change to starboard or a red rectangle for a change to port.

(b) If the length of the leg will be changed, the signal shall be the display of flag C with repetitive sounds and a '–' if the length will be decreased or a '+' if it will be increased.

(c) Subsequent legs may be changed without further signalling to maintain the course shape

34 MARK MISSING

If a *mark* is missing or out of position while boats are *racing*, the race committee shall, if possible,

(a) replace it in its correct position or substitute a new one of similar appearance, or

(b) substitute an object displaying flag M and make repetitive sound signals.

35 RACE TIME LIMIT AND SCORES

If one boat *starts*, *sails the course* and *finishes* within the time limit for that race, if any, all boats that *finish* shall be scored according to their finishing places unless the race is *abandoned*. If no boat *finishes* within the race time limit, the race committee shall *abandon* the race.

36 RACES RESTARTED OR RESAILED

If a race is restarted or resailed, a breach of a *rule* in the original race, or in any previous restart or resail of that race, shall not

(a) prohibit a boat from competing unless she has broken rule 30.4; or

(b) cause a boat to be penalized except under rule 2, 30.2, 30.4 or 69 or under rule 14 when she has caused injury or serious damage.

37 SEARCH AND RESCUE INSTRUCTIONS

When the race committee displays flag V with one sound, all boats and official and support vessels shall, if possible, monitor the race committee communication channel for search and rescue instructions.

PART 4 – OTHER REQUIREMENTS WHEN RACING

*Part 4 rules apply only to boats **racing** unless the rule states otherwise.*

Section A – General Requirements

40   PERSONAL FLOTATION DEVICES

40.1 Basic Rule

When rule 40.1 is made applicable by rule 40.2, each competitor shall wear a personal flotation device except briefly while changing or adjusting clothing or personal equipment. Wet suits and dry suits are not personal flotation devices.

40.2 When Rule 40.1 Applies

Rule 40.1 applies
(a) if flag Y was displayed afloat with one sound before or with the warning signal, while *racing* in that race; or
(b) if flag Y was displayed ashore with one sound, at all times while afloat that day.

However, rule 40.1 applies when so stated in the notice of race or sailing instructions.

41   OUTSIDE HELP   ✸*200*

A boat shall not receive help from any outside source, except
(a) help for a crew member who is ill, injured or in danger;
(b) after a collision, help from the crew of the other vessel to get clear;
(c) help in the form of information freely available to all boats;
(d) unsolicited information from a disinterested source, which may be another boat in the same race.

42   PROPULSION   ✸*200*

42.1 Basic Rule

Except when permitted in rule 42.3 or 45, a boat shall compete by using only the wind and water to increase, maintain or decrease her speed. Her crew may adjust the trim of sails and hull, and perform other acts of seamanship, but shall not otherwise move their bodies to propel the boat.

42.2 Prohibited Actions

Without limiting the application of rule 42.1, these actions are prohibited:

(a) pumping: repeated fanning of any sail either by pulling in and releasing the sail or by vertical or athwartship body movement;

(b) rocking: repeated rolling of the boat, induced by
   (1) body movement,
   (2) repeated adjustment of the sails or centreboard, or
   (3) steering;

(c) ooching: sudden forward body movement, stopped abruptly;

(d) sculling: repeated movement of the helm that is either forceful or that propels the boat forward or prevents her from moving astern;

(e) repeated tacks or gybes unrelated to changes in the wind or to tactical considerations.

42.3 Exceptions

(a) A boat may be rolled to facilitate steering.

(b) A boat's crew may move their bodies to exaggerate the rolling that facilitates steering the boat through a tack or a gybe, provided that, just after the tack or gybe is completed, the boat's speed is not greater than it would have been in the absence of the tack or gybe.

(c) When surfing (rapidly accelerating down the front of a wave), planing or foiling is possible
   (1) to initiate surfing or planing, each sail may be pulled in only once for each wave or gust of wind, or
   (2) to initiate foiling, each sail may be pulled in any number of times.

(d) When a boat is above a close-hauled course and either stationary or moving slowly, she may scull to turn to a close-hauled course.

(e) If a batten is inverted, the boat's crew may pump the sail until the batten is no longer inverted. This action is not permitted if it clearly propels the boat.

(f) A boat may reduce speed by repeatedly moving her helm.

(g) Any means of propulsion may be used to help a person or another vessel in danger.

(h) To get clear after grounding or colliding with a vessel or object, a boat may use force applied by her crew or the crew of the other vessel and any equipment other than a propulsion engine. However, the use of an engine may be permitted by rule 42.3(i).

(i) Sailing instructions may, in stated circumstances, permit propulsion using an engine or any other method, provided the boat does not gain a significant advantage in the race.

Note: Interpretations of rule 42 are available at the World Sailing website or by mail upon request.

43   EXONERATION

43.1 (a) When as a consequence of breaking a *rule* a boat has compelled another boat to break a *rule*, the other boat is exonerated for her breach.

(b) When a boat is sailing within the *room* or *mark-room* to which she is entitled and, as a consequence of an incident with a boat required to give her that *room* or *mark-room* she breaks a rule of Section A of Part 2, rule 15, 16, or 31, she is exonerated for her breach.

(c) A right-of-way boat, or one sailing within the *room* or *mark-room* to which she is entitled, is exonerated for breaking rule 14 if the contact does not cause damage or injury.   ✸*176*

43.2 A boat exonerated for breaking a *rule* need not take a penalty and shall not be penalized for breaking that *rule*.

44   PENALTIES AT THE TIME OF AN INCIDENT

44.1   Taking a Penalty   ✸*200/201*

A boat may take a Two-Turns Penalty when she may have broken one or more rules of Part 2 in an incident while *racing*. She may take a One-Turn Penalty when she may have broken rule 31. Alternatively, the notice of race or sailing instructions may specify the use of the Scoring Penalty or some other penalty, in which case the specified penalty shall replace the One-Turn and the Two-Turns Penalty. However,

(a) when a boat may have broken a rule of Part 2 and rule 31 in the same incident she need not take the penalty for breaking rule 31;

(b) if the boat caused injury or serious damage or, despite taking a penalty, gained a significant advantage in the race or series by her breach her penalty shall be to retire.

44.2   One-Turn and Two-Turns Penalties   ✸*201*

After getting well clear of other boats as soon after the incident as possible, a boat takes a One-Turn or Two-Turns Penalty by promptly making the required number of turns in the same direction, each turn including one tack and one gybe. When a boat takes the penalty at or near the finishing line, her hull shall be completely on the course side of the line before she *finishes*.

44.3 Scoring Penalty

(a) A boat takes a Scoring Penalty by displaying a yellow flag at the first reasonable opportunity after the incident.

(b) When a boat has taken a Scoring Penalty, she shall keep the yellow flag displayed until *finishing* and call the race committee's attention to it at the finishing line. At that time she shall also inform the race committee of the identity of the other boat involved in the incident. If this is impracticable, she shall do so at the first reasonable opportunity and within the protest time limit.

(c) The race score for a boat that takes a Scoring Penalty shall be the score she would have received without that penalty, made worse by the number of places stated in the notice of race or sailing instructions. When the number of places is not stated, the penalty shall be 20% of the score for Did Not *Finish*, rounded to the nearest whole number (0.5 rounded upward). The scores of other boats shall not be changed; therefore, two boats may receive the same score. However, the penalty shall not cause the boat's score to be worse than the score for Did Not *Finish*.

202 ✷ **45 HAULING OUT; MAKING FAST; ANCHORING**

A boat shall be afloat and off moorings at her preparatory signal. Thereafter, she shall not be hauled out or made fast except to bail out, reef sails or make repairs. She may anchor or the crew may stand on the bottom. She shall recover the anchor before continuing in the race unless she is unable to do so.

230 ✷ **46 PERSON IN CHARGE**

A boat shall have on board a person in charge designated by the member or organization that entered the boat. See rule 75.

47 TRASH DISPOSAL

Competitors and *support persons* shall not intentionally put trash in the water. This rule applies at all times while afloat. The penalty for a breach of this rule may be less than disqualification.

Section B – Equipment-related Requirements

48   LIMITATIONS ON EQUIPMENT AND CREW

48.1 A boat shall use only the equipment on board at her preparatory signal.

48.2 No person on board shall intentionally leave, except when ill or injured, or to help a person or vessel in danger, or to swim. A person leaving the boat by accident or to swim shall be back in contact with the boat before the crew resumes sailing the boat to the next *mark*.

49   CREW POSITION; LIFELINES

49.1 Competitors shall use no device designed to position their bodies outboard, other than hiking straps and stiffeners worn under the thighs.

49.2 When lifelines are required by the class rules or any other *rule*, competitors shall not position any part of their torsos outside them, except briefly to perform a necessary task. On boats equipped with upper and lower lifelines, a competitor sitting facing outboard with his waist inside the lower lifeline may have the upper part of his body outside the upper lifeline. Unless a class rule or any other *rule* specifies a maximum deflection, lifelines shall be taut. If the class rules do not specify the material or minimum diameter of lifelines, they shall comply with the corresponding specifications in the *World Sailing Offshore Special Regulations*.   ✸*202*

Note: Those regulations are available at the World Sailing website.

50   COMPETITOR CLOTHING AND EQUIPMENT   ✸*203*

50.1 (a) Competitors shall not wear or carry clothing or equipment for the purpose of increasing their weight.

   (b) Furthermore, a competitor's clothing and equipment shall not weigh more than 8 kilograms, excluding a hiking or trapeze harness and clothing (including footwear) worn only below the knee. Class rules or the notice of race may specify a lower weight or a higher weight up to 10 kilograms. Class rules may include footwear and other clothing worn below the knee within that weight. A hiking or trapeze harness shall have positive buoyancy and shall not weigh more than 6 kilograms. Weights shall be determined as required by Appendix H.

(c) A trapeze harness worn by a competitor which may be used to support the competitor on a trapeze shall be of the quick release variety complying with ISO 10862 which allows the competitor to detach from the hook or other method of attachment at any time. A class rule may change this rule to permit trapeze harnesses that are not of the quick release variety, but a class rule may not change the requirement that a quick release harness comply with ISO 10862.

Note: Rule 50.1(c) does not take effect until 1 January 2023.

50.2 Rules 50.1(b) and 50.1(c) do not apply to boats required to be equipped with lifelines.

203❋

51 MOVABLE BALLAST

All movable ballast, including sails that are not set, shall be properly stowed. Water, dead weight or ballast shall not be moved for the purpose of changing trim or stability. Floorboards, bulkheads, doors, stairs and water tanks shall be left in place and all cabin fixtures kept on board. However, bilge water may be bailed out.

52 MANUAL POWER

A boat's standing rigging, running rigging, spars and movable hull appendages shall be adjusted and operated only by the power provided by the crew.

53 SKIN FRICTION

A boat shall not eject or release a substance, such as a polymer, or have specially textured surfaces that could improve the character of the flow of water inside the boundary layer.

54 FORESTAYS AND HEADSAIL TACKS

Forestays and headsail tacks, except those of spinnaker staysails when the boat is not close-hauled, shall be attached approximately on a boat's centreline.

55 SETTING AND SHEETING SAILS

55.1 Changing Sails

When headsails or spinnakers are being changed, a replacing sail may be fully set and trimmed before the replaced sail is lowered. However, only one mainsail and, except when changing, only one spinnaker shall be carried set at a time.

55.2 Spinnaker Poles; Whisker Poles

Only one spinnaker pole or whisker pole shall be used at a time except when gybing. When in use, it shall be attached to the foremost mast.

55.3 Sheeting Sails

✸203

No sail shall be sheeted over or through any device that exerts outward pressure on a sheet or clew of a sail at a point from which, with the boat upright, a vertical line would fall outside the hull or deck, except:

(a) a headsail clew may be connected (as defined in *The Equipment Rules of Sailing*) to a whisker pole, provided that a spinnaker is not set;

(b) any sail may be sheeted to or led above a boom that is regularly used for a sail and is permanently attached to the mast from which the head of the sail is set;

(c) a headsail may be sheeted to its own boom that requires no adjustment when tacking; and

(d) the boom of a sail may be sheeted to a bumkin.

55.4 Headsails and Spinnakers

For the purposes of rules 54 and 55 and Appendix G, the definitions of 'headsail' and 'spinnaker' in *The Equipment Rules of Sailing* shall be used.

56 FOG SIGNALS AND LIGHTS; TRAFFIC SEPARATION SCHEMES

56.1 When so equipped, a boat shall sound fog signals and show lights as required by the *International Regulations for Preventing Collisions at Sea (IRPCAS)* or applicable government rules.

56.2 A boat shall comply with rule 10, Traffic Separation Schemes, of the *IRPCAS*.

Note: Appendix TS, Traffic Separation Schemes, is available at the World Sailing website. The notice of race may change rule 56.2 by stating that Section A, Section B or Section C of Appendix TS applies.

PART 5 – PROTESTS, REDRESS, HEARINGS, MISCONDUCT AND APPEALS

The protest form that was included in previous editions of this book has been replaced by two forms, a hearing request form and a hearing decision form. The new forms, in various formats, are available at the World Sailing website at sailing.org/racingrules/documents. *They may be downloaded and printed.*

Note that The Racing Rules of Sailing *does not require a particular form to be used.*

Suggestions for improving these forms are welcome and should be sent to rules@sailing.org.

203 ✳

Section A – Protests; Redress; Rule 69 Action

60 RIGHT TO PROTEST; RIGHT TO REQUEST REDRESS OR RULE 69 ACTION

60.1 A boat may
(a) protest another boat, but not for an alleged breach of a rule of Part 2 or rule 31 unless she was involved in or saw the incident;
(b) request redress; or
(c) report to the protest committee requesting action under rule 60.3(d) or 69.2(b).

60.2 A race committee may
(a) protest a boat, but not as a result of information arising from a request for redress or an invalid *protest*, or from a report from a person with a *conflict of interest* other than the representative of the boat herself;
(b) request redress for a boat; or
(c) report to the protest committee requesting action under rule 60.3(d) or 69.2(b).

60.3 A protest committee may
(a) protest a boat, but not as a result of information arising from a request for redress or an invalid *protest*, or from a report from a person with a *conflict of interest* other than the representative of the boat herself. However, it may protest a boat

    (1) if it learns of an incident involving her that may have resulted in injury or serious damage, or

    (2) if during the hearing of a valid *protest* it learns that the boat, although not a *party* to the hearing, was involved in the incident and may have broken a *rule*;

  (b) call a hearing to consider redress;

  (c) act under rule 69.2(b); or

  (d) call a hearing to consider whether a *support person* has broken a *rule*, based on its own observation or information received from any source, including evidence taken during a hearing.

60.4 A technical committee may

  (a) protest a boat, but not as a result of information arising from a request for redress or an invalid *protest*, or from a report from a person with a *conflict of interest* other than the representative of the boat herself. However, it shall protest a boat if it decides that a boat or personal equipment does not comply with the class rules or with rule 50;

  (b) request redress for a boat; or

  (c) report to the protest committee requesting action under rule 60.3(d) or 69.2(b).

60.5 However, neither a boat nor a committee may protest for an alleged breach of rule 69 or a Regulation referred to in rule 6, unless permitted by the Regulation concerned.

61 PROTEST REQUIREMENTS

61.1 Informing the Protestee

  (a) The protesting boat shall inform the other boat at the first reasonable opportunity. When her *protest* will concern an incident in the racing area, she shall hail 'Protest' and conspicuously display a red flag at the first reasonable opportunity for each. She shall display the flag until she is no longer *racing*. However,

    (1) if the other boat is beyond hailing distance, the protesting boat need not hail but she shall inform the other boat at the first reasonable opportunity;

    (2) if the hull length of the protesting boat is less than 6 metres, she need not display a red flag;

    (3) if the incident was an error by the other boat in *sailing the course*, she need not hail or display a red flag but she shall inform the other boat either before or at the first reasonable opportunity after the other boat *finishes*;

✱*204*

(4) if at the time of the incident it is obvious to the protesting boat that a member of either crew is in danger, or that injury or serious damage resulted, the requirements of this rule do not apply to her, but she shall attempt to inform the other boat within the time limit of rule 61.3.

(b) If the race committee, technical committee or protest committee intends to protest a boat concerning an incident the committee observed in the racing area, it shall inform her after the race within the time limit of rule 61.3. In other cases the committee shall inform the boat of its intention to protest as soon as reasonably possible. A notice posted on the official notice board within the appropriate time limit satisfies this requirement.

(c) If the protest committee decides to protest a boat under rule 60.3(a)(2), it shall inform her as soon as reasonably possible, close the current hearing, proceed as required by rules 61.2 and 63, and hear the original and the new *protests* together.

204✻

61.2 Protest Contents

A *protest* shall be in writing and identify

(a) the protestor and protestee;

(b) the incident;

(c) where and when the incident occurred;

(d) any *rule* the protestor believes was broken; and

(e) the name of the protestor's representative.

204✻

However, if requirement (b) is met, requirement (a) may be met at any time before the hearing, and requirements (d) and (e) may be met before or during the hearing. Requirement (c) may also be met before or during the hearing, provided the protestee is allowed reasonable time to prepare for the hearing.

61.3 Protest Time Limit

A *protest* by a boat, or by the race committee, technical committee or protest committee about an incident observed in the racing area, shall be delivered to the race office within the protest time limit stated in the sailing instructions. If none is stated, the time limit is two hours after the last boat in the race *finishes*. Other *protests* shall be delivered to the race office no later than two hours after the protestor receives the relevant information. The protest committee shall extend the time if there is good reason to do so.

62   REDRESS

62.1 A request for redress or a protest committee's decision to consider redress shall be based on a claim or possibility that a boat's score or place in a race or series has been or may be, through no fault of her own, made significantly worse by

✹*204*

(a) an improper action or omission of the race committee, protest committee, organizing authority or technical committee for the event, but not by a protest committee decision when the boat was a *party* to the hearing;

(b) injury or physical damage because of the action of a boat that was breaking a rule of Part 2 and took an appropriate penalty or was penalized, or of a vessel not *racing* that was required to keep clear or is determined to be at fault under the *IRPCAS* or a government right-of-way rule;

✹*204*

(c) giving help (except to herself or her crew) in compliance with rule 1.1; or

(d) an action of another boat, or a crew member or *support person* of that boat, that resulted in a penalty under rule 2 or a penalty or warning under rule 69.

62.2 A request shall be in writing and identify the reason for making it. If the request is based on an incident in the racing area, it shall be delivered to the race office within the protest time limit or two hours after the incident, whichever is later. Other requests shall be delivered as soon as reasonably possible after learning of the reasons for making the request. The protest committee shall extend the time if there is good reason to do so. No red flag is required.

✹*204*

(a) However, on the last scheduled day of racing a request for redress based on a protest committee decision shall be delivered no later than 30 minutes after the decision was posted.

Section B – Hearings and Decisions

63   HEARINGS

63.1   Requirement for a Hearing

A boat or competitor shall not be penalized without a protest hearing, except as provided in rules 30.2, 30.3, 30.4, 64.4(d), 64.5(b), 69, 78.2, A5.1 and P2. A decision on redress shall not be made without a hearing. The protest committee shall hear all *protests* and requests for redress that have been delivered to the race office unless it allows a *protest* or request to be withdrawn.

63.2 Time and Place of the Hearing; Time for Parties to Prepare

All *parties* to the hearing shall be notified of the time and place of the hearing, the *protest* or redress information or the allegations shall be made available to them, and they shall be allowed reasonable time to prepare for the hearing. When two or more hearings arise from the same incident, or from very closely connected incidents, they may be heard together in one hearing. However, a hearing conducted under rule 69 shall not be combined with any other type of hearing.

63.3 Right to Be Present

(a) A representative of each *party* to the hearing has the right to be present throughout the hearing of all the evidence. When a *protest* claims a breach of a rule of Part 2, 3 or 4, the representatives of boats shall have been on board at the time of the incident, unless there is good reason for the protest committee to rule otherwise. Any witness, other than a member of the protest committee, shall be excluded except when giving evidence.

(b) If a *party* to a hearing does not come to the hearing, the protest committee may nevertheless proceed with the hearing. If the *party* was unavoidably absent, the committee may reopen the hearing.

63.4 Conflict of Interest

(a) A protest committee member shall declare any possible *conflict of interest* as soon as he is aware of it. A *party* to the hearing who believes a member of the protest committee has a *conflict of interest* shall object as soon as possible. A *conflict of interest* declared by a protest committee member shall be included in the written information provided under rule 65.2.

(b) A member of a protest committee with a *conflict of interest* shall not be a member of the committee for the hearing, unless

(1) all *parties* consent, or

(2) the protest committee decides that the *conflict of interest* is not significant.

(c) When deciding whether a *conflict of interest* is significant, the protest committee shall consider the views of the *parties*, the level of the conflict, the level of the event, the importance to each *party*, and the overall perception of fairness.

(d) However, for World Sailing major events, or for other events as prescribed by the national authority of the venue, rule 63.4(b) does not apply and a person who has a *conflict of interest* shall not be a member of the protest committee.

63.5 Validity of the Protest or Request for Redress

At the beginning of the hearing the protest committee shall take any evidence it considers necessary to decide whether all requirements for the *protest* or request for redress have been met. If they have been met, the *protest* or request is valid and the hearing shall be continued. If not, the committee shall declare the *protest* or request invalid and close the hearing. If the *protest* has been made under rule 60.3(a)(1), the committee shall also determine whether or not injury or serious damage resulted from the incident in question. If not, the hearing shall be closed.

63.6 Taking Evidence and Finding Facts

(a) The protest committee shall take the evidence, including hearsay evidence, of the *parties* present at the hearing and of their witnesses and other evidence it considers necessary. However, the committee may exclude evidence which it considers to be irrelevant or unduly repetitive.

(b) A member of the protest committee who saw the incident shall, while the *parties* are present, state that fact and may give evidence.

(c) A *party* present at the hearing may question any person who gives evidence.

(d) The committee shall then give the weight it considers appropriate to the evidence presented, find the facts and base its decision on them.

63.7 Conflict Between Rules

If there is a conflict between two or more *rules* that must be resolved before the protest committee makes a decision, the committee shall apply the *rule* that it believes will provide the fairest result for all boats affected. Rule 63.7 applies only if the conflict is between rules in the notice of race, the sailing instructions, or any of the other documents that govern the event under item (g) of the definition *Rule*.

63.8 Hearings Involving Parties in Different Events

A hearing involving *parties* in different events conducted by different organizing authorities shall be heard by a protest committee acceptable to those authorities.

63.9 Hearings under Rule 60.3(d) — Support Persons

If the protest committee decides to call a hearing under rule 60.3(d), it shall promptly follow the procedures in rules 63.2, 63.3, 63.4 and 63.6, except that the information given to the *parties* shall be details of the alleged breach and a person may be appointed by the protest committee to present the allegation.

64 DECISIONS

64.1 Standard of Proof, Majority Decisions and Reclassifying Requests

(a) A protest committee shall make its decision based on a balance of probabilities, unless provided for otherwise in the rule alleged to have been broken.

(b) Decisions of the protest committee shall be by simple majority vote of all members. When there is equal division of votes cast, the chairman may cast an additional vote.

(c) The protest committee shall proceed with each case, as a *protest*, request for redress or other type of request, based on the information in the written request or allegation and testimony during the hearing. This permits the type of case to be changed if appropriate.

64.2 Penalties

When the protest committee decides that a boat that is a *party* to a protest hearing has broken a *rule* and is not exonerated, it shall disqualify her unless some other penalty applies. A penalty shall be imposed whether or not the applicable *rule* was mentioned in the *protest*. If a boat has broken a *rule* when not *racing*, her penalty shall apply to the race sailed nearest in time to that of the incident. However,

(a if a boat has taken an applicable penalty, she shall not be further penalized under this rule unless the penalty for a *rule* she broke is a disqualification that is not excludable from her series score;

(b) if the race is restarted or resailed, rule 36 applies.

64.3 Decisions on Redress

205 ✳

When the protest committee decides that a boat is entitled to redress under rule 62, it shall make as fair an arrangement as possible for all boats affected, whether or not they asked for redress. This may be to adjust the scoring (see rule A9 for some examples) or finishing times of boats, to *abandon* the race, to let the results stand or to make some\other arrangement. When in doubt about the facts or probable results of any arrangement for the race or series, especially before *abandoning* the race, the protest committee shall take evidence from appropriate sources.

64.4 Decisions on Protests Concerning Class Rules

(a) When the protest committee finds that deviations in excess of tolerances specified in the class rules were caused by damage or normal wear and do not improve the performance of the boat, it shall not penalize her. However, the boat shall not *race* again until the deviations have been corrected, except when the protest committee decides there is or has been no reasonable opportunity to do so.

(b) When the protest committee is in doubt about the meaning of a class rule, it shall refer its questions, together with the relevant facts, to an authority responsible for interpreting the rule. In making its decision, the committee shall be bound by the reply of the authority.

(c) When a boat is penalized under a class rule and the protest committee decides that the boat also broke the same rule in earlier races in the same event, the penalty may be imposed for all such races. No further *protest* is necessary.

✳*235*

(d) When a boat penalized under a class rule states in writing that she intends to appeal, she may compete in subsequent races without changes to the boat. However, if she fails to appeal or the appeal is decided against her, she shall be disqualified without a further hearing from all subsequent races in which she competed.

(e) Measurement costs arising from a *protest* involving a class rule shall be paid by the unsuccessful *party* unless the protest committee decides otherwise.

64.5 Decisions Concerning Support Persons

(a) When the protest committee decides that a *support person* who is a *party* to a hearing under rule 60.3(d) or 69 has broken a *rule*, it may
  (1) issue a warning,
  (2) exclude the person from the event or venue or remove any privileges or benefits, or
  (3) take other action within its jurisdiction as provided by the *rules*.

(b) The protest committee may also penalize a boat that is a *party* to a hearing under rule 60.3(d) or 69 for the breach of a *rule* by a *support person* by changing the boat's score in a single race, up to and including disqualification, when the protest committee decides that
  (1) the boat may have gained a competitive advantage as the result of the breach by the *support person*, or
  (2) the *support person* committed a further breach after the protest committee warned the boat in writing, following a previous hearing, that a penalty may be imposed.

64.6 Discretionary Penalties

When a boat reports within the protest time limit that she has broken a *rule* subject to a discretionary penalty, the protest committee shall decide the appropriate penalty after taking evidence from the boat and any witnesses it decides are appropriate.

65 INFORMING THE PARTIES AND OTHERS

65.1 After making its decision, the protest committee shall promptly inform the *parties* to the hearing of the facts found, the applicable *rules*, the decision, the reasons for it, and any penalties imposed or redress given.

65.2 A *party* to the hearing is entitled to receive the above information in writing, provided she asks for it in writing from the protest committee no later than seven days after being informed of the decision. The committee shall then promptly provide the information, including, when relevant, a diagram of the incident prepared or endorsed by the committee.

65.3 Unless there is good reason not to do so, after any hearing, including a hearing under rule 69, the protest committee may publish the information set out in rule 65.1. The protest committee may direct that the information is to be confidential to the *parties*.

65.4 When the protest committee penalizes a boat under a class rule, it shall send the above information to the relevant class rule authorities.

235

66 REOPENING A HEARING

66.1 The protest committee may reopen a hearing when it decides that it may have made a significant error, or when significant new evidence becomes available within a reasonable time. It shall reopen a hearing when required by the national authority under rule 71.2 or R5.

66.2 A *party* to the hearing may request a reopening in writing no later than 24 hours after being informed of the decision.
(a) However, on the last scheduled day of racing the request shall be delivered
  (1) within the protest time limit if the requesting *party* was informed of the decision on the previous day;
  (2) no later than 30 minutes after the *party* was informed of the decision on that day.

66.3 The protest committee shall consider all requests to reopen. When a request to reopen is being considered or the hearing is reopened,
(a) when based only on new evidence, a majority of the members of the protest committee shall, if practicable, be members of the original committee;

(b) when based on a significant error, the protest committee shall, if practicable, have at least one new member.

67 DAMAGES

The question of damages arising from a breach of any *rule* shall be governed by the prescriptions, if any, of the national authority.

Note: There is no rule 68.

Section C – Misconduct

69 MISCONDUCT

69.1 Obligation not to Commit Misconduct; Resolution

(a) A competitor, boat owner or *support person* shall not commit an act of misconduct.

(b) Misconduct is:

(1) conduct that is a breach of good manners, a breach of good sportsmanship, or unethical behaviour; or

(2) conduct that may bring, or has brought, the sport into disrepute.

(c) An allegation of a breach of rule 69.1(a) shall be resolved in accordance with the provisions of rule 69. It shall not be grounds for a *protest* and rule 63.1 does not apply.

69.2 Action by a Protest Committee

(a) A protest committee acting under this rule shall have at least three members.

(b) When a protest committee, from its own observation or from information received from any source, including evidence taken during a hearing, believes a person may have broken rule 69.1(a), it shall decide whether or not to call a hearing.

(c) When the protest committee needs more information to make the decision to call a hearing, it shall consider appointing a person or persons to conduct an investigation. These investigators shall not be members of the protest committee that will decide the matter.

(d) When an investigator is appointed, all relevant information he gathers, favourable or unfavourable, shall be disclosed to the protest committee, and if the protest committee decides to call a hearing, to the *parties*.

(e) If the protest committee decides to call a hearing, it shall promptly inform the person in writing of the alleged breach and of the time and place of the hearing and follow the procedures in rules 63.2, 63.3(a), 63.4, 63.6, 65.1, 65.2, 65.3 and 66, except that:

(1) unless a person has been appointed by World Sailing, a person may be appointed by the protest committee to present the allegation.

(2) a person against whom an allegation has been made under this rule shall be entitled to have an advisor and a representative with him who may act on his behalf.

(f) If the person

(1) provides good reason why he is unable to come to the hearing at the scheduled time, the protest committee shall reschedule it; or

(2) does not provide good reason and does not come to the hearing, the protest committee may conduct it without the person present.

235 ✸

(g) The standard of proof to be applied is the test of the comfortable satisfaction of the protest committee, bearing in mind the seriousness of the alleged misconduct. However, if the standard of proof in this rule conflicts with the laws of a country, the national authority may, with the approval of World Sailing, change it with a prescription to this rule.

(h) When the protest committee decides that a competitor or boat owner has broken rule 69.1(a), it may take one or more of the following actions

(1) issue a warning;

(2) change their boat's score in one or more races, including disqualification(s) that may or may not be excluded from her series score;

(3) exclude the person from the event or venue or remove any privileges or benefits; and

(4) take any other action within its jurisdiction as provided by the *rules*.

(i) When the protest committee decides that a *support person* has broken rule 69.1(a), rule 64.5 applies.

(j) If the protest committee

(1) imposes a penalty greater than one DNE;

(2) excludes the person from the event or venue; or

(3) in any other case if it considers it appropriate,

it shall report its findings, including the facts found, its conclusions and decision to the national authority of the person or, for specific international events listed in the World Sailing Regulations, to World Sailing. If the protest committee has acted under rule 69.2(f)(2), the report shall also include that fact and the reasons for it.

(k) If the protest committee decides not to conduct the hearing without the person present, or if the protest committee has left the event and a report alleging a breach of rule 69.1(a) is received, the race committee or organizing authority may appoint the same or a new protest committee to proceed under this rule. If it is impractical for the protest committee to conduct a hearing, it shall collect all available information and, if the allegation seems justified, make a report to the national authority of the person or, for specific international events listed in the World Sailing Regulations, to World Sailing.

69.3 Action by a National Authority and World Sailing

The disciplinary powers, procedures and responsibilities of national authorities and World Sailing that apply are specified in the World Sailing Disciplinary Code. National authorities and World Sailing may impose further penalties, including suspension of eligibility, under that code.

Section D – Appeals

70 APPEALS AND REQUESTS TO A NATIONAL AUTHORITY ✱205

70.1 (a) Provided that the right of appeal has not been denied under rule 70.5, a *party* to a hearing may appeal a protest committee's decision or its procedures, but not the facts found.

(b) A boat may appeal when she is denied a hearing required by rule 63.1.

70.2 A protest committee may request confirmation or correction of its decision.

70.3 An appeal under rule 70.1 or a request by a protest committee under rule 70.2 shall be sent to the national authority with which organizing authority is associated under rule 89.1. However, if boats will pass through the waters of more than one national authority while *racing*, an appeal or request shall be sent to the national authority where the finishing line is located, unless the sailing instructions identify another national authority.

70.4 A club or other organization affiliated to a national authority may request an interpretation of the *rules*, provided that no *protest* or request for redress that may be appealed is involved. The interpretation shall not be used for changing a previous protest committee decision.

70.5 There shall be no appeal from the decisions of an international jury constituted in compliance with Appendix N. Furthermore, if the notice of race or the sailing instructions so state, the right of appeal may be denied provided that

(a) it is essential to determine promptly the result of a race that will qualify a boat to compete in a later stage of an event or a subsequent event (a national authority may prescribe that its approval is required for such a procedure);

(b) a national authority so approves for a particular event open only to boats entered by an organization affiliated to that national authority, a member of an organization affiliated to that national authority, or a personal member of that national authority; or

(c) a national authority after consultation with World Sailing so approves for a particular event, provided the protest committee is constituted as required by Appendix N, except that only two members of the protest committee need be International Judges.

70.6 Appeals and requests shall conform to Appendix R.

71 NATIONAL AUTHORITY DECISIONS

71.1 A person who has a *conflict of interest* or was a member of the protest committee shall not take any part in the discussion or decision on an appeal or a request for confirmation or correction.

71.2 The national authority may uphold, change or reverse a protest committee's decision including a decision on validity or a decision under rule 69. Alternatively, the national authority may order that a hearing be reopened, or that a new hearing be held by the same or a different protest committee. When the national authority decides that there shall be a new hearing, it may appoint the protest committee.

71.3 When from the facts found by the protest committee the national authority decides that a boat that was a *party* to a protest hearing broke a *rule* and is not exonerated, it shall penalize her, whether or not that boat or that *rule* was mentioned in the protest committee's decision.

71.4 The decision of the national authority shall be final. The national authority shall send its decision in writing to all *parties* to the hearing and the protest committee, who shall be bound by the decision.

PART 6 – ENTRY AND QUALIFICATION

75   ENTERING AN EVENT

To enter an event, a boat shall comply with the requirements of the organizing authority of the event. She shall be entered by

(a) a member of a club or other organization affiliated to a World Sailing member national authority,

(b) such a club or organization, or

(c) a member of a World Sailing member national authority.

76   EXCLUSION OF BOATS OR COMPETITORS

76.1 The organizing authority or the race committee may reject or cancel the entry of a boat or exclude a competitor, subject to rule 76.3, provided it does so before the start of the first race and states the reason for doing so. On request the boat shall promptly be given the reason in writing. The boat may request redress if she considers that the rejection or exclusion is improper.

76.2 The organizing authority or the race committee shall not reject or cancel the entry of a boat or exclude a competitor because of advertising, provided the boat or competitor complies with World Sailing Advertising Code.

76.3 At world and continental championships no entry within stated quotas shall be rejected or cancelled without first obtaining the approval of the relevant World Sailing Class Association (or the Offshore Racing Council) or World Sailing.

77   IDENTIFICATION ON SAILS

A boat shall comply with the requirements of Appendix G governing class insignia, national letters and numbers on sails.

78   COMPLIANCE WITH CLASS RULES; CERTIFICATES   ✱*206*

78.1 While a boat is *racing*, her owner and any other person in charge shall ensure that the boat is maintained to comply with her class rules and that her measurement or rating certificate, if any, remains valid. In addition, the boat shall also comply at other times specified in the class rules, the notice of race or the sailing instructions.

78.2 When a *rule* requires a valid certificate to be produced or its existence verified before a boat *races*, and this cannot be done, the boat may *race* provided that the race committee receives a statement signed by the person in charge that a valid certificate exists. The boat shall produce the certificate or arrange for its existence to be verified by the race committee before the start of the last day of the event, or of the first series, whichever is earlier. The penalty for breaking this rule is disqualification without a hearing from all races of the event.

79 CATEGORIZATION

If the notice of race or class rules state that some or all competitors must satisfy categorization requirements, the categorization shall be carried out as described in the World Sailing Categorization Code.

80 RESCHEDULED EVENT

When an event is rescheduled to dates different from the dates stated in the notice of race, all boats entered shall be notified. The race committee may accept new entries that meet all the entry requirements except the original deadline for entries.

PART 7 – RACE ORGANIZATION

85 CHANGES TO RULES

85.1 A change to a *rule* shall refer specifically to the *rule* and state the change. A change to a *rule* includes an addition to it or deletion of all or part of it.

85.2 A change to one of the following types of *rules* may be made only as shown below.

Type of rule	Change only if permitted by
Racing rule	Rule 86
Rule in a World Sailing code	A rule in the code
National authority prescription	Rule 88.2
Class rule	Rule 87
Rule in the notice of race	Rule 89.2(b)
Rule in the sailing instructions	Rule 90.2(c)
Rule in any other document governing the event	A rule in the document itself

86 CHANGES TO THE RACING RULES

86.1 A racing rule shall not be changed unless permitted in the rule itself or as follows:

(a) Prescriptions of a national authority may change a racing rule, but not the Definitions; the Basic Principles; a rule in the Introduction; Part 1, 2 or 7; rule 42, 43, 47, 50, 63.4, 69, 70, 71, 75, 76.3 or 79; a rule of an appendix that changes one of these rules; Appendix H or N; or a rule in a World Sailing Code listed in rule 6.1.

(b) The notice of race or sailing instructions may change a racing rule, but not rule 76.1 or 76.2, Appendix R, or a rule listed in rule 86.1(a).

(c) Class rules may change only racing rules 42, 49, 51, 52, 53, 54 and 55.

86.2 In exception to rule 86.1, World Sailing may in limited circumstances (see World Sailing Regulation 28.1.3) authorize changes to the racing rules for a specific international event. The authorization shall be stated in a letter of approval to the organizing authority and in the notice of race or sailing instructions, and the letter shall be posted on the official notice board.

86.3 If a national authority so prescribes, the restrictions in rule 86.1 do not apply if rules are changed to develop or test proposed rules. The national authority may prescribe that its approval is required for such changes.

87 CHANGES TO CLASS RULES

The notice of race may change a class rule only when the class rules permit the change, or when written permission of the class association for the change is posted on the official notice board.

88 NATIONAL PRESCRIPTIONS

88.1 Prescriptions that apply

The prescriptions that apply to an event are the prescriptions of the national authority with which the organizing authority is associated under rule 89.1. However, if boats will pass through the waters of more than one national authority while *racing*, the notice of race shall identify the prescriptions that will apply and when they will apply.

88.2 Changes to Prescriptions

The notice of race or sailing instructions may change a prescription. However, a national authority may restrict changes to its prescriptions with a prescription to this rule, provided

World Sailing approves its application to do so. The restricted prescriptions shall not be changed.

89 ORGANIZING AUTHORITY; NOTICE OF RACE; APPOINTMENT OF RACE OFFICIALS

89.1 Organizing Authority

Races shall be organized by an organizing authority, which shall be

(a) World Sailing;

(b) a member national authority of World Sailing;

(c) an affiliated club;

(d) an affiliated organization other than a club and, if so prescribed by the national authority, with the approval of the national authority or in conjunction with an affiliated club;

(e) an unaffiliated class association, either with the approval of the national authority or in conjunction with an affiliated club;

(f) two or more of the above organizations;

(g) an unaffiliated body in conjunction with an affiliated club where the body is owned and controlled by the club. The national authority of the club may prescribe that its approval is required for such an event; or

(h) if approved by World Sailing and the national authority of the club, an unaffiliated body in conjunction with an affiliated club where the body is not owned and controlled by the club.

In rule 89.1, an organization is affiliated if it is affiliated to the national authority of the venue; otherwise the organization is unaffiliated. However, if boats will pass through the waters of more than one national authority while *racing*, an organization is affiliated if it is affiliated to the national authority of one of the ports of call.

89.2 Notice of Race; Appointment of Race Officials

206✳

(a) The organizing authority shall publish a notice of race that conforms to rule J1. The notice of race may be changed provided adequate notice is given.

(b) The notice of race may be changed provided adequate notice is given.

(c) The organizing authority shall appoint a race committee and, when appropriate, appoint a protest committee, a technical committee and umpires. However, the race committee, an international jury, a technical committee and umpires may be appointed by World Sailing as provided in its Regulations.

90 RACE COMMITTEE; SAILING INSTRUCTIONS; SCORING

90.1 Race Committee

The race committee shall conduct races as directed by the organizing authority and as required by the *rules*.

90.2 Sailing Instructions

(a) The race committee shall publish written sailing instructions that conform to rule J2.

(b) When appropriate, for an event where entries from other countries are expected, the sailing instructions shall include, in English, the applicable national prescriptions.

(c) The sailing instructions may be changed provided the change is in writing and posted on the official notice board before the time stated in the sailing instructions or, on the water, communicated to each boat before her warning signal. Oral changes may be given only on the water, and only if the procedure is stated in the sailing instructions.

❋*206/ 207*

❋*207*

90.3 Scoring

(a) The race committee shall score a race or series as provided in Appendix A unless the notice of race or sailing instructions specify some other system. A race shall be scored if it is not *abandoned* and if one boat *starts*, *sails the course* and *finishes* within the race time limit, if any, even if she retires after *finishing* or is disqualified.

(b) When a scoring system provides for excluding one or more race scores, any score that is a Disqualification Not Excludable (DNE) shall be included in a boat's series score.

(c) When the race committee determines from its own records or observations that it has scored a boat incorrectly, it shall correct the error and make the corrected scores available to competitors.

(d) The race committee shall implement scoring changes directed by the protest committee or national authority as a result of decisions made in accordance with the *rules*.

(e) When so stated in the notice of race, notwithstanding the provisions of rules 90.3(a), (b), (c) and (d), there shall be no changes to race or series scores resulting from action, including the correction of errors, initiated more than 24 hours after

(1) the protest time limit for the last race of the series (including a single-race series);

(2) being informed of a protest committee decision after the last race of the series (including a single-race series); or

(3) the results are published.

However, in exception, changes to scores shall be made resulting from a decision under rules 6, 69 or 70. The notice of race may change '24 hours' to a different time.

91 PROTEST COMMITTEE

A protest committee shall be

(a) a committee appointed by the organizing authority or race committee;

(b) an international jury appointed by the organizing authority or as prescribed in the World Sailing Regulations. It shall be composed as required by rule N1 and have the authority and responsibilities stated in rule N2. A national authority may prescribe that its approval is required for the appointment of international juries for races within its jurisdiction, except World Sailing events or when international juries are appointed by World Sailing under rule 89.2(c); or

(c) a committee appointed by the national authority under rule 71.2.

92 TECHNICAL COMMITTEE

92.1 A technical committee shall be a committee of at least one member and be appointed by the organizing authority or the race committee or as prescribed in the World Sailing Regulations.

92.2 The technical committee shall conduct equipment inspection and event measurement as directed by the organizing authority and as required by the *rules*.

APPENDIX A – SCORING

See rule 90.3.

A1 NUMBER OF RACES

The number of races scheduled and the number required to be completed to constitute a series shall be stated in the notice of race or sailing instructions.

A2 SERIES SCORES

A2.1 Each boat's series score shall, subject to rule 90.3(b), be the total of her race scores excluding her worst score. However, the notice of race or sailing instructions may make a different arrangement by providing, for example, that no score will be excluded, that two or more scores will be excluded, or that a specified number of scores will be excluded if a specified number of races are completed. A race is completed if scored; see rule 90.3(a). If a boat has two or more equal worst scores, the score(s) for the race(s) sailed earliest in the series shall be excluded. The boat with the lowest series score wins and others shall be ranked accordingly.

A2.2 If a boat has entered any race in a series, she shall be scored for the whole series.

A3 STARTING TIMES AND FINISHING PLACES

✱237

The time of a boat's starting signal shall be her starting time, and the order in which boats *finish* a race shall determine their finishing places. However, when a handicap or rating system is used a boat's corrected time shall determine her finishing place.

A4 SCORING SYSTEM

This Low Point System will apply unless the notice of race or sailing instructions specify another system; see rule 90.3(a).

Each boat *starting* and *finishing* and not thereafter retiring, being penalized or given redress shall be scored points as follows:

Finishing place	Points
First	1
Second	2
Third	3
Fourth	4
Fifth	5
Sixth	6
Seventh	7
Each place thereafter	Add 1 point

A5 SCORES DETERMINED BY THE RACE COMMITTEE

A5.1 A boat that did not *start*, *sail the course* or *finish*, or comply with rule 30.2, 30.3, 30.4 or 78.2, or that retires or takes a penalty under rule 44.3(a), shall be scored accordingly by the race committee without a hearing. Only the protest committee may take other scoring actions that worsen a boat's score.

A5.2 A boat that did not *start*, did not *sail the course*, did not *finish*, retired or was disqualified shall be scored points for the finishing place one more than the number of boats entered in the series. A boat that is penalized under rule 30.2 or that takes a penalty under rule 44.3(a) shall be scored points as provided in rule 44.3(c).

A5.3 If the notice of race or sailing instructions state that rule A5.3 will apply, rule A5.2 is changed so that a boat that came to the starting area but did not *start*, did not *sail the course*, did not *finish*, retired or was disqualified shall be scored points for the finishing place one more than the number of boats that came to the starting area, and a boat that did not come to the starting area shall be scored points for the finishing place one more than the number of boats entered in the series.

A6   CHANGES IN PLACES AND SCORES OF OTHER BOATS

A6.1 If a boat is disqualified from a race or retires after *finishing*, each boat with a worse finishing place shall be moved up one place.

A6.2 If the protest committee decides to give redress by adjusting a boat's score, the scores of other boats shall not be changed unless the protest committee decides otherwise.

A7   RACE TIES

If boats are tied at the finishing line or if a handicap or rating system is used and boats have equal corrected times, the points for the place for which the boats have tied and for the place(s) immediately below shall be added together and divided equally. Boats tied for a race prize shall share it or be given equal prizes.

A8   SERIES TIES

A8.1 If there is a series-score tie between two or more boats, each boat's race scores shall be listed in order of best to worst, and at the first point(s) where there is a difference the tie shall be broken in favour of the boat(s) with the best score(s). No excluded scores shall be used.

A8.2 If a tie remains between two or more boats, they shall be ranked in order of their scores in the last race. Any remaining ties shall be broken by using the tied boats' scores in the next-to-last race and so on until all ties are broken. These scores shall be used even if some of them are excluded scores.

A9 GUIDANCE ON REDRESS

If the protest committee decides to give redress by adjusting a boat's score for a race, it is advised to consider scoring her

(a) points equal to the average, to the nearest tenth of a point (0.05 to be rounded upward), of her points in all the races in the series except the race in question;

(b) points equal to the average, to the nearest tenth of a point (0.05 to be rounded upward), of her points in all the races before the race in question; or

(c) points based on the position of the boat in the race at the time of the incident that justified redress.

A10 SCORING ABBREVIATIONS

These scoring abbreviations shall be used for recording the circumstances described:

DNC Did not *start*; did not come to the starting area

DNS Did not *start* (other than DNC and OCS)

OCS Did not *start*; on the course side of the starting line at her starting signal and failed to *start*, or broke rule 30.1

ZFP 20% penalty under rule 30.2

UFD Disqualification under rule 30.3

BFD Disqualification under rule 30.4

SCP Scoring Penalty applied

NSC Did not *sail the course*

DNF Did not *finish*

RET Retired

DSQ Disqualification

DNE Disqualification that is not excludable

RDG Redress given

DPI Discretionary penalty imposed

APPENDIX B – WINDSURFING FLEET RACING RULES

Windsurfing fleet races (including marathon races) shall be sailed under The Racing Rules of Sailing *as changed by this appendix. The term 'boat' elsewhere in the racing rules means 'board' or 'boat' as appropriate. A marathon race is a race intended to last more than one hour.*

Note: Rules for Slalom, Expression (including Wave and Freestyle) and Speed disciplines are not included in this appendix. These are available at the World Sailing website.

CHANGES TO THE DEFINITIONS

The definitions *Mark-Room*, and *Tack, Starboard* or *Port* are changed to:

Mark-Room *Mark-Room* for a board is *room* to sail her *proper course* to round or pass the *mark*. However, *mark-room* for a board does not include *room* to tack unless she is *overlapped* inside and to *windward* of the board required to give *mark-room* and she would be *fetching* the *mark* after her tack.

Tack, Starboard or **Port** A board is on the *tack, starboard* or *port*, corresponding to the competitor's hand that would be nearer the mast if the competitor were in normal sailing position with both hands on the wishbone and arms not crossed. A board is on *starboard tack* when the competitor's right hand would be nearer the mast and is on *port tack* when the competitor's left hand would be nearer the mast.

The definition *Zone* is deleted.

Add the following definitions:

Capsized A board is *capsized* when she is not under control because her sail or the competitor is in the water.

Rounding or Passing A board is *rounding* or *passing* a *mark* from the time her *proper course* is to begin to manoeuvre to round or pass it, until the *mark* has been rounded or passed.

B1 CHANGES TO THE RULES OF PART 1
[No changes.]

B2 CHANGES TO THE RULES OF PART 2

13 WHILE TACKING

Rule 13 is changed to:

After a board passes head to wind, she shall *keep clear* of other boards until her sail has filled. During that time rules 10, 11 and 12 do not apply. If two boards are subject to this rule at the same time, the one on the other's port side or the one astern shall *keep clear*.

17 ON THE SAME TACK BEFORE A REACHING START

Rule 17 is changed to:

When, at the warning signal, the course to the first *mark* is approximately ninety degrees from the true wind, a board *overlapped* to *leeward* of another board on the same *tack* during the last 30 seconds before her starting signal shall not sail above her *proper course* while they remain *overlapped* if as a result the other board would need to take action to avoid contact, unless in doing so she promptly sails astern of the other board.

18 MARK-ROOM

Rule 18 is changed as follows:

The first sentence of rule 18.1 is changed to:

Rule 18 applies between boards when they are required to leave a mark on the same side and at least one of them is rounding or passing it.

Rule 18.2(b) is changed to:

(b) If boards are *overlapped* when the first of them is *rounding or passing* the *mark*, the outside board at that moment shall thereafter give the inside board *mark-room*. If a board is *clear ahead* when she is *rounding or passing* the *mark*, the board *clear astern* at that moment shall thereafter give her *mark-room*.

Rule 18.2(c) is changed to:

(c) When a board is required to give *mark-room* by rule B2.18.2(b), she shall continue to do so even if later an *overlap* is broken or a new *overlap* begins. However, if the board entitled to *mark-room* passes head to wind, rule B2.18.2(b) ceases to apply.

Rule 18.2(d) is changed to:

(d) Rules 18.2(b) and (c) cease to apply if the board entitled to *mark-room* passes head to wind.

Rule 18.3 is deleted.

18.4 Gybing or Bearing Away

Rule 18.4 is changed to:

When an inside *overlapped* right-of-way board must gybe or bear away at a *mark* to sail her *proper course*, until she gybes or bears away she shall sail no farther from the *mark* than needed to sail that course. Rule 18.4 does not apply at a gate *mark*.

22 CAPSIZED; AGROUND; RESCUING

Rule 22 is changed to:

22.1 If possible, a board shall avoid a board that is *capsized* or has not regained control after *capsizing*, is aground, or is trying to help a person or vessel in danger.

22.2 If possible, a board that is *capsized* or aground shall not interfere with another board.

23 INTERFERING WITH ANOTHER BOARD; SAIL OUT OF WATER

Add new rule 23.3:

23.3 In the last minute before her starting signal, a board shall have her sail out of the water and in a normal position, except when accidentally *capsized*.

B3 CHANGES TO THE RULES OF PART 3

26 STARTING RACES

Rule 26 is changed to:

26.1 System 1 (for Upwind Starts)

Races shall be started by using the following signals. Times shall be taken from the visual signals; the absence of a sound signal shall be disregarded.

Minutes before starting signal	Visual signal	Sound signal	Means
5*	Class flag	One	Warning signal
4	P, I, U, or black flag	One	Preparatory signal
1	Preparatory flag removed	One long	One minute
0	Class flag removed	One	Starting signal

*or as stated in the notice of race or sailing instructions

The warning signal for each succeeding class shall be made with or after the starting signal of the preceding class.

26.2 System 2 (for Reaching Starts)

Races shall be started by using the following signals. Times shall be taken from the visual signals; the absence of a sound signal shall be disregarded.

Minutes before starting signal	Visual signal	Sound signal	Means
3	Class flag		Attention signal
2	Red flag; attention signal removed	One	Warning signal
1	Yellow flag; red flag removed	One	Preparatory signal
½	Yellow flag removed		30 seconds
0	Green flag	One	Starting signal

26.3 System 3 (for Beach Starts)

(a) When the starting line is on the beach, or so close to the beach that the competitor must stand in the water to *start*, the start is a beach start.

(b) The starting stations shall be numbered so that station 1 is the most windward one. Unless the sailing instructions specify some other system, a board's starting station shall be determined
   (1) by ranking (the highest ranking board on station 1, the next highest on station 2, and so on), or
   (2) by draw.

(c) After boards have been called to take their positions, the race committee shall make the preparatory signal by displaying a red flag with one sound. The starting signal shall be made, at any time after the preparatory signal, by removing the red flag with one sound.

(d) After the starting signal each board shall take the shortest route from her starting station to the water and then to her sailing position without interfering with other boards. Part 2 rules will apply when both of the competitor's feet are on the board.

30   STARTING PENALTIES
Rule 30.2 is deleted.

31   TOUCHING A MARK
Rule 31 is changed to:
A board may touch a *mark* but shall not hold on to it.

B4   CHANGES TO THE RULES OF PART 4

42   PROPULSION
Rule 42 is changed to:
A board shall be propelled only by the action of the wind on the sail and by the action of the water on the hull. However, pumping and fanning the sail is permitted. The board shall not be propelled by paddling, swimming or walking.

44   PENALTIES AT THE TIME OF AN INCIDENT
Rule 44 is changed to:

44.1   Taking a Penalty
A board may take a 360°-Turn Penalty when she may have broken one of more rules of Part 2 in an incident while *racing*. The sailing instructions may specify the use of some other penalty. However, if the board caused injury or serious damage or, despite taking a penalty, gained a significant advantage in the race or series by her breach, her penalty shall be to retire.

44.2   360°-Turn Penalty
After getting well clear of other boards as soon after the incident as possible, a board takes a 360°-Turn Penalty by promptly making a 360° turn with no requirement for a tack or a gybe. When a board takes the penalty at or near the finishing line, her hull shall be completely on the course side of the line before she *finishes*.

50   COMPETITOR CLOTHING AND EQUIPMENT
Rule 50.1(a) is changed to:
(a) Competitors shall not wear or carry clothing or equipment for the purpose of increasing their weight. However, a competitor may wear a drinking container that shall have a capacity of no more than 1.5 litres.

PART 4 RULES DELETED
Rules 45, 48.2, 49, 50.1(c), 50.2, 51, 52, 54, 55 and 56.1 are deleted.

B5   CHANGES TO THE RULES OF PART 5

60   RIGHT TO PROTEST; RIGHT TO REQUEST REDRESS OR RULE 69 ACTION

Rule 60.1(a) is changed by deleting 'or saw'.

61   PROTEST REQUIREMENTS

61.1 Informing the Protestee

Rule 61.1(a) is changed to:

(a) The protesting board shall inform the other board at the first reasonable opportunity. When her *protest* will concern an incident in the racing area, she shall hail 'Protest' at the first reasonable opportunity. She shall also inform the race committee of her intention to protest as soon as practicable after she *finishes* or retires. However,

    (1) if the other board is beyond hailing distance, the protesting board need not hail but she shall inform the other board at the first reasonable opportunity;

    (2) no red flag need be displayed;

    (3) if the incident was an error by the other board in *sailing the course*, she need not hail but she shall inform the other board either before or at the first reasonable opportunity after the other board *finishes*;

    (4) if at the time of the incident it is obvious to the protesting board that either competitor is in danger, or that injury or serious damage resulted, the requirements of this rule do not apply to her, but she shall attempt to inform the other board within the time limit of rule 61.3.

61.2 Protest Contents

Add to rule 61.2:

This rule does not apply to a race in an elimination series that will qualify a board to compete in a later stage of an event.

62   REDRESS

Rule 62.1(b) is changed to:

(b) injury, physical damage or *capsize* because of the action of

    (1) a board that broke a rule of Part 2 and took an appropriate penalty or was penalized, or

    (2) a vessel not *racing* that was required to keep clear.

63 HEARINGS

63.6 Taking Evidence and Finding Facts

Add to rule 63.6:

However, for an elimination series race that will qualify a board to compete in a later stage of an event, *protests* and requests for redress need not be in writing; they shall be made orally to a member of the protest committee as soon as reasonably possible following the race. The protest committee may take evidence in any way it considers appropriate and may communicate its decision orally.

64 DECISIONS

Rule 64.4(b) is changed to:

(b) When the protest committee is in doubt about a matter concerning the measurement of a board, the meaning of a class rule, or damage to a board, it shall refer its questions, together with the relevant facts, to an authority responsible for interpreting the rule. In making its decision, the committee shall be bound by the reply of the authority.

65 INFORMING THE PARTIES AND OTHERS

Add to rule 65.2:

This rule does not apply to a race in an elimination series that will qualify a board to compete in a later stage of an event.

70 APPEALS AND REQUESTS TO A NATIONAL AUTHORITY

Rules 70.5 and 70.5(a) are changed to:

70.5 There shall be no appeal from the decisions of an international jury constituted in compliance with Appendix N, and no appeal from the decisions of the protest committee for a race in an elimination series that will qualify a board to compete in a later stage of an event. Furthermore, if the notice of race or sailing instructions so state, the right of appeal may be denied provided that

(a) it is essential to determine promptly the result of a race that will qualify a board to compete in a a subsequent event (a national authority may prescribe that its permission is required for such a procedure);

B6 CHANGES TO THE RULES OF PART 6

78 COMPLIANCE WITH CLASS RULES; CERTIFICATES

Add to rule 78.1: 'When so prescribed by World Sailing, a numbered and dated device on a board and her centreboard, fin and rig shall serve as her measurement certificate.'

B7 CHANGES TO THE RULES OF PART 7

90 RACE COMMITTEE; SAILING INSTRUCTIONS; SCORING

The last sentence of rule 90.2(c) is changed to: 'Oral instructions may be given only if the procedure is stated in the sailing instructions.'

B8 CHANGES TO APPENDIX A

A1 NUMBER OF RACES; OVERALL SCORES

Rule A1 is changed to:

The number of races scheduled and the number required to be completed to constitute a series shall be stated in the notice of race or sailing instructions. If an event includes more than one discipline or format, the notice of race or sailing instructions shall state how the overall scores are to be calculated.

A2.1 SERIES SCORES

Rule A2.1 is changed to:

Each board's series score shall, subject to rule 90.3(b), be the total of her race scores excluding her

(a) worst score when from 5 to 11 races have been completed, or

(b) two worst scores when 12 or more races have been completed.

However, the notice of race or sailing instructions may make a different arrangement. A race is completed if scored; see rule 90.3(a). If a board has two or more equal worst scores, the score(s) for the race(s) sailed earliest in the series shall be excluded. The board with the lowest series score wins and others shall be ranked accordingly.

A5 SCORES DETERMINED BY THE RACE COMMITTEE

Add new rule A5.4:

A5.4 For an elimination series race that will qualify a board to compete in a later stage of an event, a board that did not *start*, did not *sail the course*, did not *finish*, retired or was disqualified shall be scored points equal to the number of boards permitted to sail in that race.

A8 SERIES TIES

Rule A8 is changed to:

A8.1 If there is a series-score tie between two or more boards, each board's excluded race scores shall be listed in order of best to worst, and at the first point(s) where there is a difference the tie shall be broken in favour of the board(s) with the best excluded race score(s).

A8.2 If a tie remains between two or more boards, each board's race scores, including excluded scores, shall be listed in order of best to worst, and at the first point(s) where there is a difference the tie shall be broken in favour of the board(s) with the best score(s). These scores shall be used even if some of them are excluded scores.

A8.3 If a tie still remains between two or more boards, they shall be ranked in order of their scores in the last race. Any remaining ties shall be broken by using the tied boards' scores in the next-to-last race and so on until all ties are broken. These scores shall be used even if some of them are excluded scores.

B9   CHANGES TO APPENDIX G

G1   WORLD SAILING CLASS BOARDS

G1.3 Postioning

Rule G1.3 is changed to:

The class insignia shall be displayed once on each side of the sail in the area above a line projected at right angles from a point on the luff of the sail one-third of the distance from the head to the wishbone. The national letters and sail numbers shall be in the central third of that part of the sail above the wishbone, clearly separated from any advertising. They shall be black and applied back to back on an opaque white background. The background shall extend a minimum of 30 mm beyond the characters. There shall be a '–' between the national letters and the sail number, and the spacing between characters shall be adequate for legibility.

APPENDIX G RULES DELETED

Rules G1.2(a)(2) and G1.2(a)(3) are deleted.

APPENDIX C – MATCH RACING RULES

Match races shall be sailed under The Racing Rules of Sailing *as changed by this appendix. Matches shall be umpired unless the notice of race or sailing instructions state otherwise.*

Note: A Standard Notice of Race, Standard Sailing Instructions, and Match Racing Rules for Blind Competitors are available at the World Sailing website.

C1 TERMINOLOGY

'Competitor' means the skipper, team or boat as appropriate for the event. 'Flight' means two or more matches started in the same starting sequence.

C2 CHANGES TO THE DEFINITIONS AND THE RULES OF PARTS 1, 2, 3 AND 4

C2.1 The definition *Finish* is changed to:

Finish A boat *finishes* when any part of her hull crosses the finishing line from the course side after completing any penalties. However, when penalties are cancelled under rule C7.2(d) after one or both boats have *finished* each shall be recorded as *finished* when she crossed the line. A boat has not *finished* if she continues to *sail the course*.

C2.2 The definition *Mark-Room* is changed to:

Mark-Room *Room* for a boat to sail her *proper course* to round or pass the *mark*, and *room* to pass a finishing *mark* after *finishing*.

C2.3 Add to the definition *Proper Course*: 'A boat taking a penalty or manoeuvring to take a penalty is not sailing a *proper course*.'

C2.4 In the definition *Zone* the distance is changed to two hull lengths.

C2.5 Add new rule 7 to Part 1:

7 LAST POINT OF CERTAINTY

The umpires will assume that the state of a boat, or her relationship to another boat, has not changed, until they are certain that it has changed.

C2.6 Rule 13 is changed to:

13 WHILE TACKING OR GYBING

13.1 After a boat passes head to wind, she shall *keep clear* of other boats until she is on a close-hauled course.

13.2 After the foot of the mainsail of a boat sailing downwind crosses the centreline she shall *keep clear* of other boats until her mainsail has filled or she is no longer sailing downwind.

13.3 While rule 13.1 or 13.2 applies, rules 10, 11 and 12 do not. However, if two boats are subject to rule 13.1 or 13.2 at the same time, the one on the other's port side or the one astern shall *keep clear*.

C2.7 Rule 16.2 is deleted.

C2.8 Rule 17 is deleted.

C2.9 Rule 18 is changed to:

18 MARK-ROOM

18.1 When Rule 18 Applies

Rule 18 applies between boats when they are required to leave a *mark* on the same side and at least one of them is in the *zone*. However, it does not apply between a boat approaching a *mark* and one leaving it. Rule 18 no longer applies between boats when the boat entitled to *mark-room* is on the next leg and the *mark* is astern of her.

18.2 Giving Mark-Room

(a) When the first boat reaches the *zone*,
  (1) if boats are *overlapped*, the outside boat at that moment shall thereafter give the inside boat *mark-room*.
  (2) if boats are not *overlapped*, the boat that has not reached the *zone* shall thereafter give *mark-room*.
(b) If the boat entitled to *mark-room* leaves the *zone*, the entitlement to *mark-room* ceases and rule 18.2(a) is applied again if required based on the relationship of the boats at the time rule 18.2(a) is re-applied.
(c) If a boat obtained an inside *overlap* and, from the time the *overlap* began, the outside boat is unable to give *mark-room*, she is not required to give it.

18.3 Tacking or Gybing

(a) If *mark-room* for a boat includes a change of *tack*, such tack or gybe shall be done no faster than a tack or gybe to sail her *proper course*.

(b) When an inside *overlapped* right-of-way boat must change *tack* at a *mark* to sail her *proper course*, until she changes *tack* she shall sail no farther from the *mark* than needed to sail that course. Rule 18.3(b) does not apply at a gate *mark* or a finishing *mark* and a boat shall be exonerated for breaking this rule if the course of another boat was not affected before the boat changed *tack*.

C2.10 Rule 20.4(a) is changed to:

(a) The following arm signals by the helmsman are required in addition to the hails:

(1) for *room* to tack, repeatedly and clearly pointing to windward; and

(2) for 'You tack', repeatedly and clearly pointing at the other boat and waving the arm to windward.

C2.11 Rule 21.3 is deleted.

C2.12 Rule 23.1 is changed to:

23.1 If reasonably possible, a boat not *racing* shall not interfere with a boat that is *racing* or an umpire boat.'

C2.13 Add new rule 23.3:

23.3 When boats in different matches meet, any change of course by either boat shall be consistent with complying with a *rule* or trying to win her own match.'

C2.14 Rule 31 is changed to:

31 TOUCHING A MARK

While *racing*, neither the crew nor any part of a boat's hull shall touch a starting *mark* before *starting*, a *mark* that begins, bounds or ends the leg of the course on which she is sailing, or a finishing *mark* after *finishing*. In addition, while *racing*, a boat shall not touch a race committee vessel that is also a *mark*.

C2.15 Add new rule 41(e):

(e) help to recover from the water and return on board a crew member, provided the return on board is at the approximate location of the recovery.

C2.16 Rule 42 shall also apply between the warning and preparatory signals.

C2.17 Rule 42.2(d) is changed to:

(e) sculling: repeated movement of the helm to propel the boat forward;

C3 RACE SIGNALS AND CHANGES TO RELATED RULES

C3.1 Starting Signals

The signals for starting a match shall be as follows. Times shall be taken from the visual signals; the failure of a sound signal shall be disregarded. If more than one match will be sailed, the starting signal for one match shall be the warning signal for the next match.

Time in minutes	Visual signal	Sound signal	Means
7	Flag F displayed	One	Attention signal
6	Flag F removed	None	
5	Numeral pennant displayed*	One	Warning signal
4	Flag P displayed	One	Preparatory signal
2	Blue or yellow flag or both displayed**	One**	End of pre-start entry time
1	Flag P removed	One long	
0	Warning signal removed	One	Starting signal

*Within a flight, numeral pennant 1 means Match 1, pennant 2 means Match 2, etc., unless the sailing instructions state otherwise.
**These signals shall be made only if one or both boats fail to comply with rule C4.2. The flag(s) shall be displayed until the umpires have signalled a penalty or for one minute, whichever is earlier.

C3.2 Changes to Related Rules

(a) Rule 29.1 is changed to:

(1) When at a boat's starting signal any part of her hull is on the course side of the starting line or one of its extensions, the race committee shall promptly display a blue or yellow flag identifying the boat with one sound. The flag shall be displayed until the hull of the boat is completely on the pre-start side of the starting line or one of its extensions or until two minutes after her starting signal, whichever is earlier.

(2) When after a boat's starting signal any part of her hull from the pre-start side to the course side of the starting line across an extension without having *started* correctly, the race committee shall promptly display a blue or yellow flag identifying the boat. The flag shall be displayed until

the hull of the boat is completely on the pre-start side of the starting line or one of its extensions or until two minutes after her starting signal, whichever is earlier.

(b) In the race signal AP the last sentence is changed to: 'The attention signal will be made 1 minute after removal unless at that time the race is *postponed* again or *abandoned*.'

(c) In the race signal N the last sentence is changed to: 'The attention signal will be made 1 minute after removal unless at that time the race is *abandoned* again or *postponed*.'

C3.3 Finishing Line Signals
The race signal Blue flag or shape shall not be used.

C4 REQUIREMENTS BEFORE THE START

C4.1 At a boat's preparatory signal, her hull shall be completelyoutside the line that is at a 90° angle to the starting line through the starting *mark* at her assigned end. In the pairing list, the boat listed on the left-hand side is assigned the port end and shall display a blue flag at her stern while *racing*. The other boat is assigned the starboard end and shall display a yellow flag at her stern while *racing*.

C4.2 Within the two-minute period following a boat's preparatory signal, her hull shall cross and clear the starting line, the first time from the course side to the pre-start side.

C5 SIGNALS BY UMPIRES

C5.1 A green and white flag with one long sound means 'No penalty'.

C5.2 A blue or yellow flag identifying a boat with one long sound means 'The identified boat shall take a penalty by complying with rule C7.'

C5.3 A red flag with or soon after a blue or yellow flag with one long sound means 'The identified boat shall take a penalty by complying with rule C7.3(d).'

C5.4 A black flag with a blue or yellow flag and one long sound means 'The identified boat is disqualified, and the match is terminated and awarded to the other boat.'

C5.5 One short sound means 'A penalty is now completed.'

C5.6 Repetitive short sounds mean 'A boat is no longer taking a penalty and the penalty remains.'

C5.7 A blue or yellow flag or shape displayed from an umpire boat means 'The identified boat has an outstanding penalty.'

C6 PROTESTS AND REQUESTS FOR REDRESS BY BOATS

C6.1 A boat may protest another boat

(a) under a rule of Part 2, except rule 14, by clearly displaying flag Y immediately after an incident in which she was involved;

(b) under any rule not listed in rule C6.1(a) or C6.2 by clearly displaying a red flag as soon as possible after the incident.

C6.2 A boat may not protest another boat under

(a) rule 14, unless damage or injury results;

(b) a rule of Part 2, unless she was involved in the incident;

(c) rule 31 or 42; or

(d) rule C4 or C7.

C6.3 A boat requesting redress because of circumstances that arise while she is *racing* or in the finishing area, shall clearly display a red flag as soon as possible after she becomes aware of those circumstances, but no later than two minutes after *finishing* or retiring.

C6.4 (a) A boat protesting under rule C6.1(a) shall remove flag Y before or as soon as possible after the umpires' signal.

(b) A boat protesting under rule C6.1(b) or requesting redress under rule C6.3 shall, for her *protest* or request to be valid, keep her red flag displayed until she has so informed the umpires after *finishing* or retiring. No written *protest* or request for redress is required.

C6.5 Umpire Decisions

(a) After flag Y is displayed, the umpires shall decide whether to penalize any boat. They shall signal their decision in compliance with rule C5.1, C5.2 or C5.3. However,

(1) if the umpires decide to penalize a boat, and as a result that boat will have more than two outstanding penalties, the umpires shall signal her disqualification under rule C5.4;

(2) when the umpires penalize a boat under rule C8.2 and in the same incident there is a flag Y from a boat, the umpires may disregard the flag Y.

(b) The red-flag penalty in rule C5.3 shall be used when a boat has gained a controlling position as a result of breaking a *rule*, but the umpires are not certain that the conditions for an additional umpire-initiated penalty have been fulfilled.

C6.6 Protest Committee Decisions

(a) The protest committee may take evidence in any way it considers appropriate and may communicate its decision orally.

(b) If the protest committee decides that a breach of a *rule* has had no significant effect on the outcome of the match, it may
  (1) impose a penalty of one point or part of one point;
  (2) order a resail; or
  (3) make another arrangement it decides is equitable, which may be to impose no penalty.
(c) The penalty for breaking rule 14 when damage or injury results will be at the discretion of the protest committee, and may include exclusion from further races in the event.

C6.7 Add new rule N1.10 to Appendix N:
N1.10 In rule N.1, one International Umpire may be appointed to the jury, or a panel of it, in place of one International Judge.

C7   PENALTY SYSTEM

C7.1 Deleted Rule
Rule 44 is deleted.

C7.2 All Penalties
(a) A penalized boat may delay taking a penalty within the limitations of rule C7.3 and shall take it as follows:
  (1) When on a leg of the course to a windward *mark*, she shall gybe and, as soon as reasonably possible, luff to a close-hauled course.
  (2) When on a leg of the course to a leeward *mark* or the finishing line, she shall tack and, as soon as reasonably possible, bear away to a course that is more than ninety degrees from the true wind.
(b) Add to rule 2: 'When *racing*, a boat need not take a penalty unless signalled to do so by an umpire.'
(c) A boat completes a leg of the course when any part of her hull crosses the extension of the line from the previous *mark* through the *mark* she is rounding, or on the last leg when she *finishes*.
(d) A penalized boat shall not be recorded as having finished until she takes her penalty and her hull is completely on the course side of the line and she then *finishes*, unless the penalty is cancelled before or after she crosses the finishing line.
(e) If a boat has one or two outstanding penalties and the other boat in her match is penalized, one penalty for each boat shall be cancelled except that a red-flag penalty shall not cancel or be cancelled by another penalty.
(f) If one boat has *finished* and is no longer *racing*, and the other boat has an outstanding penalty, the umpires may cancel the outstanding penalty.

C7.3 Penalty Limitations

(a) A boat taking a penalty that includes a tack shall have the spinnaker head below the main-boom gooseneck from the time she passes head to wind until she is on a close-hauled course.

(b) No part of a penalty may be taken inside the *zone* of a rounding *mark* that begins, bounds or ends the leg the boat is on.

(c) If a boat has one outstanding penalty, she may take the penalty any time after starting and before finishing. If a boat has two outstanding penalties, she shall take one of them as soon as reasonably possible, but not before starting.

(d) When the umpires display a red flag with or soon after a penalty flag, the penalized boat shall take a penalty as soon as reasonably possible, but not before starting.

C7.4 Taking and Completing Penalties

(a) When a boat with an outstanding penalty is on a leg to a windward *mark* and gybes, or is on a leg to a leeward *mark* or the finishing line and passes head to wind, she is taking a penalty.

(b) When a boat taking a penalty either does not take the penalty correctly or does not complete the penalty as soon as reasonably possible, she is no longer taking a penalty. The umpires shall signal this as required by rule C5.6.

(c) The umpire boat for each match shall display blue or yellow flags or shapes, each flag or shape indicating one outstanding penalty. When a boat has taken a penalty, or a penalty has been cancelled, one flag or shape shall be removed, with the appropriate sound signal. Failure of the umpires to signal correctly shall not change the number of penalties outstanding.

C8   PENALTIES INITIATED BY UMPIRES

C8.1 Rule Changes

Rules 60.2(a) and 60.3(a) do not apply to *rules* for which penalties may be imposed by umpires.

C8.2 When the umpires decide that a boat has broken rule 31, 42, C4, C7.3(c) or C7.3(d) she shall be penalized by signalling her under rule C5.2 or C5.3. However, if a boat is penalized for breaking a rule of Part 2 and if she in the same incident breaks rule 31, she shall not be penalized for breaking rule 31. Furthermore, a boat that displays an incorrect flag or does not display the correct flag shall be warned orally and given an opportunity to correct the error before being penalized.

C8.3 When the umpires decide that a boat has
   (a) gained an advantage by breaking a *rule* after allowing for a penalty,
   (b) deliberately broken a *rule*, or
   (c) committed a breach of sportsmanship,
   she shall be penal-ized under rule C5.2, C5.3 or C5.4.

C8.4 If the umpires or protest committee members decide that a boat may have broken a *rule* other than those listed in rules C6.1(a) and C6.2, they shall so inform the protest committee for its action under rule 60.3 and rule C6.6 when appropriate.

C8.5 When, after one boat has *started*, the umpires are satisfied that the other boat will not *start*, they may signal under rule C5.4 that the boat that did not *start* is disqualified and the match is terminated.

C8.6 When the match umpires, together with at least one other umpire, decide that a boat has broken rule 14 and damage resulted, they may impose a points-penalty without a hearing. The competitor shall be informed of the penalty as soon as practicable and, at the time of being so informed, may request a hearing. The protest committee shall then proceed under rule C6.6. Any penalty decided by the protest committee may be more than the penalty imposed by the umpires. When the umpires decide that a penalty greater than one point is appropriate, they shall act under rule C8.4.

C9 REQUESTS FOR REDRESS OR REOPENING; APPEALS; OTHER PROCEEDINGS

C9.1 There shall be no request for redress or an appeal from a decision made under rule C5, C6, C7 or C8. In rule 66 the third sentence is changed to: 'A *party* to the hearing may not ask for a reopening.'

C9.2 A competitor may not base a request for redress on a claim that an action by an official boat was improper. The protest committee may decide to consider giving redress in such circumstances but only if it believes that an official boat, including an umpire boat, may have seriously interfered with a competing boat.

C9.3 No proceedings of any kind may be taken in relation to any action or non-action by the umpires, except as permitted in rule C9.2.

C10   SCORING

C10.1 The winning competitor of each match scores one point (half a point each for a dead heat); the loser scores no points.

C10.2 When a competitor withdraws from part of an event the scores of all completed races shall stand.

C10.3 When a single round robin is terminated before completion, or a multiple round robin is terminated during the first round robin, a competitor's score shall be the average points scored per match sailed by the competitor. However, if any of the competitors have completed less than one third of the scheduled matches, the entire round robin shall be disregarded and, if necessary, the event declared void. For the purposes of tie-breaking in rule C11.1(a), a competitor's score shall be the average points scored per match between the tied competitors.

C10.4 When a multiple round robin is terminated with an incomplete round robin, only one point shall be available for all the matches sailed between any two competitors, as follows:

Number of matches completed between any two competitors	Points for each win
1	One point
2	Half a point
3	A third of a point

(etc.)

C10.5 **In a round-robin series,**
   (a) competitors shall be placed in order of their total scores, highest score first;
   (b) a competitor who has won a match but is disqualified for breaking a *rule* against a competitor in another match shall lose the point for that match (but the losing competitor shall not be awarded the point); and
   (c) the overall position between competitors who have sailed in different groups shall be decided by the highest score.

C10.6 In a knockout series the sailing instructions shall state the minimum number of points required to win a series between two competitors. When a knockout series is terminated it shall be decided in favour of the competitor with the higher score.

C10.7 When only one boat in a match fails to *sail the course*, she shall be scored no points (without a hearing).

C11 TIES

C11.1 Round-Robin Series

In a round-robin series competitors are assigned to one or more groups and scheduled to sail against all other competitors in their group one or more times. Each separate stage identified in the event format shall be a separate round-robin series irrespective of the number of times each competitor sails against each other competitor in that stage.

Ties between two or more competitors in a round-robin series shall be broken by the following methods, in order, until all ties are broken. When one or more ties are only partially broken, rules C11.1(a) to C11.1(e) shall be reapplied to them. Ties shall be decided in favour of the competitor(s) who

(a) placed in order, has the highest score in the matches between the tied competitors;

(b) when the tie is between two competitors in a multiple round robin, has won the last match between the two competitors;

(c) has the most points against the competitor placed highest in the round-robin series or, if necessary, second highest, and so on until the tie is broken. When two separate ties have to be resolved but the resolution of each depends upon resolving the other, the following principles shall be used in the rule C11.1(c) procedure:

　(1) the higher-place tie shall be resolved before the lower-place tie, and

　(2) all the competitors in the lower-place tie shall be treated as a single competitor for the purposes of rule C11.1(c);

(d) after applying rule C10.5(c), has the highest place in the different groups, irrespective of the number of competitors in each group;

(e) has the highest place in the most recent stage of the event (fleet race, round robin, etc.).

C11.2 Knockout Series

Ties (including 0–0) between competitors in a knockout series shall be broken by the following methods, in order, until the tie is broken. The tie shall be decided in favour of the competitor who

(a) has the highest place in the most recent round-robin series, applying rule C11.1 if necessary;

(b) has won the most recent match in the event between the tied competitors.

C11.3 Remaining Ties

When rule C11.1 or C11.2 does not resolve a tie,

(a) if the tie needs to be resolved for a later stage of the event (or another event for which the event is a direct qualifier), the tie shall be broken by a sail-off when practicable. When the race committee decides that a sail-off is not practicable, the tie shall be decided in favour of the competitor who has the highest score in the round-robin series after eliminating the score for the first race for each tied competitor or, should this fail to break the tie, the second race for each tied competitor and so on until the tie is broken. When a tie is partially resolved, the remaining tie shall be broken by reapplying rule C11.1 or C11.2.

(b) to decide the winner of an event that is not a direct qualifier for another event, or the overall position between competitors eliminated in one round of a knockout series, a sail-off may be used (but not a draw).

(c) when a tie is not broken any monetary prizes or ranking points for tied places shall be added together and divided equally among the tied competitors.

APPENDIX D – TEAM RACING RULES

Team races shall be sailed under The Racing Rules of Sailing *as changed by this appendix.*

D1   CHANGES TO THE RACING RULES

D1.1   Definitions and the Rules of Parts 2 and 4

(a) In the definition *Zone* the distance is changed to two hull lengths.

(b) Rule 18.2(b) is changed to:

If boats are *overlapped* when the first of them reaches the *zone*, the outside boat at that moment shall thereafter give the inside boat *mark-room*. If a boat is *clear ahead* when she reaches the *zone*, or she later becomes *clear ahead* when another boat passes head to wind, the boat *clear astern* at that moment shall thereafter give her *mark-room*.

(c) Rule 18.4 is deleted.

(d) When stated in the sailing instructions, rule 20 is changed so that the following arm signals are required in addition to the hails:

    (1) for *room* to tack, repeatedly and clearly pointing to windward; and

    (2) for 'You tack', repeatedly and clearly pointing at the other boat and waving the arm to windward.

(e) Rule 23.1 is changed to: 'If reasonably possible, a boat not *racing* shall not interfere with a boat that is *racing*, and a boat that has *finished* shall not act to interfere with a boat that has not *finished*.'

(f) Add new rule 23.3: 'When boats in different races meet, any change of course by either boat shall be consistent with complying with a *rule* or trying to win her own race.'

(g) Add to rule 41:

    (e) help from another boat on her team provided electronic communication is not used.

(h) Rule 45 is deleted.

D1.2 Protests and Requests for Redress

(a) Rule 60.1 is changed to:

    A boat may

    (a) protest another boat, but not for an alleged breach of a rule of Part 2 unless she was involved in the incident or the incident involved contact between members of the other team; or

    (b) request redress.

(b) Rule 61.1(a) is changed so that the boat may remove her red flag after it has been conspicuously displayed.

(c) The boat requesting redress for an incident in the racing area shall display a red flag at the first reasonable opportunity after the incident. She shall display the red flag until it is acknowledged by the race committee or by an umpire.

(d) The race committee or protest committee shall not protest a boat for breaking a rule of Part 2 or rule 31 or 42 except

    (1) based on evidence in a report from an umpire after a black and white flag has been displayed; or

    (2) under rule 14 upon receipt of a report from any source alleging damage or injury.

(e) *Protests* and requests for redress need not be in writing. The protest committee may take evidence in any way it considers appropriate and may communicate its decision orally.

(f) A boat is not entitled to redress based on damage or injury caused by another boat on her team.

(g) When a supplied boat suffers a breakdown, rule D5 applies.

D1.3 Penalties

(a) Rule 44.1 is changed to:

A boat may take a One-Turn Penalty when she may have broken one or more rules of Part 2, or rule 31 or 42, in an incident while *racing*. However, when she may have broken a rule of Part 2 and rule 31 in the same incident she need not take the penalty for breaking rule 31.

(b) When a boat clearly indicates that she will take a penalty under rule 44.1, she shall take that penalty.

(c) A boat may take a penalty by retiring and informing the race committee or an umpire.

(d) There shall be no penalty for breaking a rule of Part 2 when the incident is between boats on the same team and there is no contact.

D2 UMPIRED RACES

D2.1 When Rule D2 Applies

Rule D2 applies to umpired races. Races to be umpired shall be identified in the notice of race or sailing instructions or by the display of flag J no later than the warning signal.

D2.2 Protests by Boats

When a boat protests under a rule of Part 2 or under rule 31 or 42 for an incident in the racing area, she is not entitled to a hearing and the following applies:

(a) She shall hail 'Protest' and conspicuously display a red flag at the first reasonable opportunity for each.

(b) The boats shall be given time to respond.

(c) If no boat takes a penalty or clearly indicates that she will do so, an umpire shall decide whether to penalize any boat.

(d) If more than one boat breaks a *rule*, an umpire shall decide whether to penalize any boat that did not take a penalty.

(e) An umpire shall signal a decision in compliance with rule D2.4.

D2.3 Penalties Initiated by an Umpire

An umpire may penalize a boat without a *protest* by another boat, or report the incident to the protest committee, or both, when the boat

(a) breaks rule 31 or 42 and does not take a penalty;

(b) breaks a rule of Part 2 and makes contact with another boat on her team or with a boat in another race, and no boat takes a penalty;

(c) breaks a *rule* and her team gains an advantage despite her, or another boat on her team, taking a penalty;

(d) breaks rule 14 and there is damage or injury;

(e) breaks rule D1.3(b);

(f) fails to take a penalty signalled by an umpire;

(g) commits a breach of sportsmanship.

The umpire shall signal a decision in compliance with rule D2.4.

D2.4 Signals by an Umpire

An umpire shall signal a decision with one long sound and the display of a flag as follows:

(a) For no penalty, a green and white flag.

(b) To penalize one or more boats, a red flag. The umpire shall hail or signal to identify each boat penalized.

(c) To report the incident to the protest committee, a black and white flag.

D2.5 Penalties Imposed by Umpires

A boat penalized by an umpire shall take a Two-Turns Penalty. However, when a penalty is imposed under rule D2.3 and an umpire hails or signals a number of turns, the boat shall take that number of One-Turn Penalties.

D2.6 Limitations on Other Proceedings

(a) A breach of rule D2.5 shall not be grounds for a protest by a boat.

(b) A decision, action or non-action of an umpire shall not be
    (1) grounds for redress,
    (2) subject to an appeal under rule 70, or
    (3) grounds for *abandoning* a race after it has started.

(c) The protest committee may decide to consider giving redress when it believes that an official boat, including an umpire boat, may have seriously interfered with a competing boat.

D3 SCORING A RACE

D3.1
(a) Each boat *finishing* a race and not retiring thereafter shall be scored points equal to her finishing place. All other boats shall be scored points equal to the number of boats entitled to *race*.

(b) When a boat is scored OCS, 10 points shall be added to her score unless she retired as soon as possible after the starting signal.

(c) When a boat fails to take a penalty imposed by an umpire at or near the finishing line, she shall be scored as retired.

(d) When a boat is scored as retired after *finishing*, each boat with a worse finishing place shall be moved up one place.

(e) When a protest committee decides that a boat that is a *party* to a protest hearing has broken a *rule* and is not exonerated,

    (1) if the boat has not taken a penalty, 6 points shall be added to her score;

    (2) if the boat's team has gained an advantage despite any penalty taken or imposed, the boat's score may be increased;

    (3) when the boat has broken rule 1 or 2, rule 14 when she has caused damage or injury, or a *rule* when not *racing*, half or more race wins may be deducted from her team, or no penalty may be imposed. Race wins deducted shall not be awarded to any other team.

D3.2 When all boats on one team have *finished*, retired or failed to *start*, the other team's boats *racing* at that time shall be scored the points they would have received had they *finished*.

D3.3 The team with the lower total points wins the race. If the totals are equal, the team that does not have first place wins.

D4 SCORING AN EVENT

D4.1 Terminology
    (a) The format of an event consists of one or more stages.

    (b) In a round-robin stage, teams are divided into one or more groups, and each group is scheduled to sail one or more round-robins.

    (c) A round-robin consists of each team in a group sailing one race against each other team in that group.

    (d) A knock-out stage consists of one or more rounds in which each team sails one match. A match is one or more races between two teams.

D4.2 Event Format
    (a) The sailing instructions shall state the format and stages of the event, and any special scoring rules.

    (b) In order to conclude an event, the race committee may change or terminate any part of the format at any reasonable time taking into account the entries, weather, time constraints and other relevant factors.

D4.3 Scoring a Round-Robin Stage
    (a) Teams in a round-robin group shall be ranked in order of number of race wins, highest first. If the teams have not completed an equal number of races, they shall be ranked in order of the percentage of races won, highest first.

    (b) However, if a round-robin is terminated when fewer than 80% of its scheduled races have been completed, its race results shall not be included, but shall be used to break ties between teams in the group who all sailed each other in the terminated round-robin.

(c) Results from a previous round-robin stage shall only be carried forward if stated in the sailing instructions.

D4.4 Round-Robin Tie Breaks

Ties in a round-robin stage shall be broken using results from that stage only.

(a) If the tied teams have all sailed each other at least once in the stage, the tie shall be broken in the order below.

(1) Percentage of races won in all races between the tied teams, highest first;

(2) Average points per race in all races between the tied teams, lowest first;

(3) If two teams remain tied, the winner of the last race between them;

(4) Average points per race in all races against common opponents, lowest first;

(5) A sail-off if possible, otherwise a game of chance.

(b) Otherwise, the tie shall be broken using only steps (4) and (5) above.

(c) When a tie is partially broken by one of the above, the remaining tie shall be broken in accordance with D4.4(a) or (b) as appropriate.

D4.5 Scoring a Knock-Out Stage

(a) A round shall not be scored unless at least one race has been completed in each match in that round. The final and petit-final are separate rounds.

(b) The winner of a match shall be the first team to score the number of race wins stated in the sailing instructions. If a match is terminated, the winner shall be the team with the higher number of race wins in that match or, if this is a tie, the team that won the last race of the match.

(c) (1) Teams that win in a round shall be ranked ahead of those that lose.

(2) Teams that lose in a round and do not sail again shall be equally ranked.

(3) In a round that is not scored, teams shall be ranked in order of their places in the previous stage of the event, with teams from different groups ranked separately.

D5 BREAKDOWNS WHEN BOATS ARE SUPPLIED BY THE ORGANIZING AUTHORITY

D5.1 Rule D5 applies when boats are supplied by the organizing authority.

D5.2 When a boat suffers a breakdown in the racing area, she may request a score change by displaying a red flag at the first reasonable opportunity after the breakdown until it is acknowledged by the race committee or by an umpire. If possible, she shall continue *racing*.

D5.3 The race committee shall decide requests for a score change in accordance with rules D5.4 and D5.5. It may take evidence in any way it considers appropriate and may communicate its decision orally.

D5.4 When the race committee decides that the team's finishing position was made significantly worse, that the breakdown was through no fault of the crew, and that in the same circumstances a reasonably competent crew would not have been able to avoid the breakdown, it shall make as equitable a decision as possible. This may be to *abandon* and resail the race or, when the boat's finishing position was predictable, award her points for that position. Any doubt about a boat's position when she broke down shall be resolved against her.

D5.5 A breakdown caused by defective supplied equipment or a breach of a *rule* by an opponent shall not normally be determined to be the fault of the crew, but one caused by careless handling, capsizing or a breach by a boat on the same team shall be. If there is doubt, it shall be presumed that the crew are not at fault.

APPENDIX E – RADIO SAILING RACING RULES

Radio sailing races shall be sailed under The Racing Rules of Sailing *as changed by this appendix.*

Note: A Test Rule for Umpired Radio Sailing is available at the World Sailing website.

E1 CHANGES TO THE DEFINITIONS, TERMINOLOGY AND THE RULES OF PARTS 1, 2 AND 7

E1.1 Definitions

Add to the definition *Conflict of Interest*:
However, an observer does not have a *conflict of interest* solely by being a competitor.

In the definition *Zone* the distance is changed to four hull lengths.

Add new definition:
Disabled A boat is *disabled* while she is unable to continue in the heat.

E1.2 Terminology

The Terminology paragraph of the Introduction is changed so that:

(a) 'Boat' means a sailboat controlled by radio signals and having no crew. However, in the rules of Part 1 and Part 5, rule E6 and the definitions *Party* and *Protest*, 'boat' includes the competitor controlling her.

(b) 'Competitor' means the person designated to control a boat using radio signals.

(c) In the racing rules, but not in its appendices, replace the noun 'race' with 'heat'. In Appendix E a race consists of one or more heats and is completed when the last heat in the race is completed.

E1.3 Rules of Parts 1, 2 and 7

(a) Rule 1.2 is deleted.

(b) Hails under rules 20.1 and 20.3 shall include the words 'room' and 'tack' and the sail number of the hailing boat, in any order

(c) Rule 22 is changed to: 'If possible, a boat shall avoid a boat that is *disabled*.'

(d) Rule 90.2(c) is changed to:

Changes to the sailing instructions may be communicated orally to all affected competitors before the warning signal of the relevant race or heat. When appropriate, changes shall be confirmed in writing.

E2 ADDITIONAL RULES WHEN RACING

Rule E2 applies only while boats are racing.

E2.1 Hailing Requirements

(a) A hail shall be made and repeated as appropriate so that the competitors to whom the hail is directed might reasonably be expected to hear it.

(b) When a *rule* requires a boat to hail or respond, the hail shall be made by the competitor controlling the boat.

(c) The individual digits of a boat's sail number shall be hailed; for example 'one five', not 'fifteen'.

E2.2 Giving Advice

A competitor shall not give tactical or strategic advice to a competitor controlling a boat that is *racing*.

E2.3 Boat Out of Radio Control

A competitor who loses radio control of his boat shall promptly hail '(The boat's sail number) out of control' and the boat shall retire.

E2.4 Transmitter Aerials

If a transmitter aerial is longer than 200mm when extended, the extremity shall be adequately protected.

E2.5 Radio Interference

Transmission of radio signals that cause interference with the control of other boats is prohibited. A competitor that has broken this rule shall not *race* again until permitted to do so by the race committee.

E3 CONDUCT OF A RACE

E3.1 Control Area

Unless the sailing instructions specify a control area, it shall be unrestricted. Competitors shall be in this area when controlling boats that are *racing*, except briefly to handle and then release or relaunch the boat.

E3.2 Launching Area

Unless the sailing instructions specify a launching area and its use, it shall be unrestricted.

E3.3 Course Board

When the sailing instructions require a course board to be displayed, it shall be located in or adjacent to the control area.

E3.4 Starting and Finishing

(a) Rule 26 is changed to:

Heats shall be started using warning, preparatory and starting signals at one-minute intervals. During the minute before the starting signal, additional sound or oral signals shall be made at ten-second intervals, and during the final ten seconds at one-second intervals. Each signal shall be timed from the beginning of its sound.

(b) The starting and finishing lines shall be between the course sides of the starting and finishing *marks*.

E3.5 Individual Recall

Rule 29.1 is changed to:

When at a boat's starting signal any part of her hull is on the course side of the starting line or when she must comply with rule 30.1, the race committee shall promptly hail 'Recall (sail numbers)'. If rule 30.3 or 30.4 applies this rule does not.

E3.6 General Recall

Rule 29.2 is changed to:

When at the starting signal the race committee is unable to identify boats that are on the course side of the starting line or to which rule 30 applies, or there has been an error in the starting procedure, the race committee may hail 'General recall' and make two loud sounds. The warning signal for a new start will normally be made shortly thereafter.

E3.7 U Flag and Black Flag Rules

When the race committee informs a boat that she has broken rule 30.3 or 30.4, the boat shall immediately leave the course area.

E3.8 Other Changes to the Rules of Part 3

(a) Rules 30.2 and 33 are deleted.

(b) All race committee signals shall be made orally or by other sounds. No visual signals are required unless specified in the sailing instructions.

(c) Courses shall not be shortened.

(d) Rule 32.1(a) is changed to: 'because of foul weather or thunderstorms,'.

E3.9 Disabled Competitors

The race committee may make or permit reasonable arrange-
ments to assist disabled competitors to compete on as equal
terms as possible. A boat or the competitor controlling her that
receives any such assistance, including help from a *support
person*, does not break rule 41.

E4 RULES OF PART 4

E4.1 Deleted Rules in Part 4

Rules 40, 44.3, 45, 48, 49, 50, 52, 54, 55 and 56 are deleted.

E4.2 Outside Help

Rule 41 is changed to:

A boat or the competitor controlling her shall not receive help
from any outside source, except

(a) help needed as a direct result of a competitor becoming ill,
injured or in danger;

(b) when the boat is entangled with another boat, help from the
other competitor;

(c) when the boat is *disabled* or in danger, help from the race
committee;

(d) help in the form of information freely available to all
competitors;

(e) unsolicited information from a disinterested source. A
competitor is not a disinterested source unless acting as an
observer.

E4.3 Taking a Penalty

Rule 44.1 is changed to:

A boat may take a One-Turn Penalty when she may have broken
one or more rules of Part 2, or rule 31, in an incident while
racing. However,

(a) when she may have broken a rule of Part 2 and rule 31 in
the same incident she need not take the penalty for breaking
rule 31;

(b) if the boat gained an advantage in the heat or race by
her breach despite taking a penalty, her penalty shall be
additional One-Turn Penalties until her advantage is lost;

(c) if the boat caused serious damage, or as a result of breaking
a rule of Part 2 she caused another boat to become *disabled*
and retire, her penalty shall be to retire.

E4.4 Person in Charge

Rule 46 is changed to: 'The member or organization that
entered the boat shall designate the competitor. See rule 75.'

E5 RACING WITH OBSERVERS AND UMPIRES

E5.1 Observers

(a) The race committee may appoint observers, who may be competitors.

(b) Observers shall hail the sail numbers of boats that make contact with a *mark* or another boat.

(c) At the end of a heat, observers shall report to the race committee all unresolved incidents, and any failure to *sail the course*.

E5.2 Rules for Observers and Umpires

Observers and umpires shall be located in the control area. They shall not use any aid or device that gives them a visual advantage over competitors.

E6 PROTESTS AND REQUESTS FOR REDRESS

E6.1 Right to Protest

Rule 60.1 is changed to:

A boat may

(a) protest another boat, but not for an alleged breach of a rule of Part 2, 3 or 4 unless she was scheduled to sail in that heat; or

(b) request redress.

However, a boat or competitor may not protest for an alleged breach of rules E2 or E3.7.

E6.2 Protest for a Rule Broken by a Competitor

When a race committee, protest committee or technical committee learns that a competitor may have broken a *rule*, it may protest the boat controlled by that competitor.

E6.3 Informing the Protestee

Rule 61.1(a) is changed to:

The protesting boat intending shall inform the other boat at the first reasonable opportunity. When her *protest* concerns an incident in the racing area, she shall hail '(Her own sail number) protest (the sail number of the other boat)'.

E6.4 Informing the Race Committee

The boat protesting or requesting redress about an incident while *racing* shall inform the race committee as soon as reasonably possible after *finishing* or retiring.

E6.5 Time Limits

A *protest*, request for redress or request for reopening shall be delivered to the race committee no later than ten minutes after the last boat in the heat *finishes* or after the relevant incident, whichever is later.

E6.6 Redress

Add to rule 62.1:

(e) external radio interference acknowledged by the race committee, or

(f) becoming *disabled* because of the action of a boat that was breaking a rule of Part 2 or of a vessel not *racing* that was required to keep clear.

E6.7 Right to Be Present

In rule 63.3(a) 'the representatives of boats shall have been on board' is changed to 'the representative of each boat shall be the competitor designated to control her'.

E6.8 Taking Evidence and Finding Facts

Add new rule 63.6(e):

(e) When the *protest* concerns an alleged breach of a rule of Part 2, 3 or 4, any witness shall have been in the control area at the time of the incident. If the witness is a competitor who was not acting as an observer, he shall also have been scheduled to race in the relevant heat.

E6.9 Decisions on Redress

Add to rule 64.3:

If a boat is given redress because she was damaged, her redress shall include reasonable time, but not more than 30 minutes, to make repairs before her next heat.

E7 PENALTIES

When a protest committee decides that a boat that is a *party* to a protest hearing has broken a *rule* other than a rule of Part 2, 3 or 4, it shall either

(a) disqualify her or add any number of points (including zero and fractions of points) to her score. The penalty shall be applied, if possible, to the heat or race in which the *rule* was broken; otherwise it shall be applied to the next heat or race for that boat. When points are added, the scores of other boats shall not be changed; or

(b) require her to take one or more One-Turn Penalties that shall be taken as soon as possible after the starting signal of her next heat that is started and not subsequently recalled or *abandoned*.

However, if the boat has broken a rule in Appendix G or rule E8, the protest committee shall act in accordance with rule G4.

E8 CHANGES TO APPENDIX G, IDENTIFICATION ON SAILS
Rule G1, except the table of National Sail Letters, is changed to:

G1 WORLD SAILING AND IRSA CLASS BOATS
This rule applies to every boat of a class administered or recognised by World Sailing or by the International Radio Sailing Association (IRSA).

G1.1 Identification
(a) A boat of a World Sailing or IRSA Class shall display her class insignia, national letters and sail number as specified in rule G1, unless her class rules state otherwise.

(b) At world and continental championships, sails shall comply with these rules. At other events they shall comply with these rules or the rules applicable at the time of their initial certification.

G1.2 National Letters
At all international events, a boat shall display national letters in accordance with the table of National Sail Letters denoting:

(a) when entered under rule 75(a), the national authority of the nationality, place of residence, or affiliation of the owner or the member.

(b) when entered under rule 75(b), the national authority of the organisation which entered her.

For the purposes of this rule, international events are world and continental championships and events described as international events in their notices of race and sailing instructions.

Note: An up-to-date version of the National Sail Letters table is available on the World Sailing website.

G1.3 Sail numbers
(a) The sail number shall be the last two digits of the boat's registration number or the competitor's or owner's personal number, allotted by the relevant issuing authority.

(b) When there is conflict between sail numbers, or when a sail number may be misread, the race committee shall require that the sail numbers of one or more boats be changed to numeric alternatives.

G1.4 Specifications
(a) National letters and sail numbers shall be in capital letters and Arabic numerals, clearly legible and of the same colour. Commercially available typefaces giving the same or better legibility than Helvetica are acceptable.

(b) The height and spacing of letters and numbers shall be as follows:

Dimension	Minimum	Maximum
Height of sail numbers	100 mm	110 mm
Spacing of adjacent sail numbers	20 mm	30 mm
Height of national letters	60 mm	70 mm
Spacing of adjacent national letters	13 mm	23 mm

G1.5 Positioning

(a) Class insignia, sail numbers and national letters shall be positioned
   (1) on both sides of the sail;
   (2) with those on the starboard side uppermost;
   (3) approximately horizontally;
   (4) with no less than 40 mm vertical spacing between numbers and letters on opposite sides of the sail;
   (5) with no less than 20 mm vertical spacing between class insignia on opposite sides of the sail.
   However, symmetrical or reversed class insignia may be positioned back to back.

(b) On a mainsail, sail numbers shall be positioned
   (1) below class insignia;
   (2) above the line perpendicular to the luff through the quarter leech point;
   (3) above national letters;
   (4) with sufficient space in front of the sail number for a prefix '1'.

G1.6 Exceptions

(a) Where the size of the sail prevents compliance with rule G1.2, National Letters, then exceptions to rules G1.2, G1.4, and G1.5 shall be made in the following order of precedence. National letters shall
   (1) be spaced vertically below sail numbers by less an 30 mm, but no less than 20 mm;
   (2) be spaced on opposite sides of the sail by less than 30 mm, but no less than 20 mm;
   (3) be reduced in height to less than 45 mm, but no less than 40 mm;
   (4) be omitted.

(b) Where the size of the sail prevents compliance with rule G1.3, Sail Numbers, then exceptions to rules G1.4 and G1.5

shall be made in the following order of precedence. Sail numbers shall
(1) extend below the specified line;
(2) be spaced on opposite sides of the sail by less than 30 mm, but no less than 20 mm apart;
(3) be reduced in height to less than 90 mm, but no less than 80 mm;
(4) be omitted on all except the largest sail;
(5) be reduced in height until they do fit on the largest sail.

APPENDIX F – KITEBOARDING RACING RULES

Kiteboard course races shall be sailed under The Racing Rules of Sailing *as changed by this appendix. The term 'boat' elsewhere in the racing rules means 'kiteboard' or 'boat' as appropriate.*

Note: Rules for other kiteboard racing formats (such as Short Track, Kitecross, Slalom, Boarder X) or other kiteboard competitions (such as Freestyle, Wave, Big Air, Speed) are not included in this appendix. Links to current versions of these rules can be found on the World Sailing website.

CHANGES TO THE DEFINITIONS
The definitions *Clear Astern* and *Clear Ahead*; *Overlap*, *Finish*, Keep *Clear*, *Leeward* and *Windward*, Mark-Room, *Obstruction*, *Start*, *Tack*, *Starboard* or *Port* and *Zone* are changed to:

Clear Astern and Clear Ahead; **Overlap** One kiteboard is *clear astern* of another when her hull is behind a line abeam from the aftermost point of the other kiteboard's hull. The other kiteboard is *clear ahead*. They *overlap* when neither is *clear astern*. However, they also *overlap* when a kiteboard between them *overlaps* both. If there is reasonable doubt that two kiteboards are overlapped, it shall be presumed that they are not. These terms always apply to kiteboards on the same *tack*. They apply to kiteboards on opposite *tacks* only when both kiteboards are sailing more than ninety degrees from the true wind.

Finish A kiteboard *finishes* when, after *starting*, while the competitor is in contact with the hull, any part of her hull, or the competitor, crosses the finishing line from the course side. However, she has not *finished* if after crossing the finishing line she

(a) takes a penalty under rule 44.2,

(b) corrects an error in *sailing the course* made at the line, or

(c) continues to *sail the course*.

Keep Clear A kiteboard *keeps clear* of a right-of-way kiteboard

(a) if the right-of-way kiteboard can sail her course with no need to take avoiding action and,

(b) when the kiteboards are *overlapped*, if the right-of-way kiteboard can also change course in both directions or move her kite in any direction without immediately making contact.

Leeward and **Windward** A kiteboard's *leeward* side is the side that is or, when she is head to wind, was away from the wind. However, when sailing by the lee or directly downwind, her *leeward* side is the side on which her kite lies. The other side is her *windward* side. When two kiteboards on the same *tack overlap*, the one whose hull is on the *leeward* side of the other's hull is the *leeward* kiteboard. The other is the *windward* kiteboard.

Mark-Room *Room* for a kiteboard to sail her *proper course* to round or pass the *mark* on the required side.

Obstruction An object that a kiteboard could not pass without substantially changing her course or the position of her kite, if she were sailing directly towards it and 10 metres from it. An object that can be safely passed on only one side and an object, area or line so designated by the sailing instructions are also *obstructions*. However, a kiteboard *racing* is not an *obstruction* to other kiteboards unless they are required to *keep clear* of her or, if rule 22 applies, avoid her. A vessel under way, including a kiteboard *racing*, is never a continuing *obstruction*.

Start A kiteboard *starts* when, her hull and the competitor having been entirely on the pre-start side of the starting line at or after her starting signal, and having complied with rule 30.1 if it applies, any part of her hull, or the competitor crosses the starting line from the pre-start side to the course side.

Tack, Starboard or **Port** A kiteboard is on the *tack*, *starboard* or *port*, corresponding to the competitor's hand that would be forward if the competitor were in normal riding position (riding heel side with both hands on the control bar and arms not crossed). A kiteboard is on *starboard tack* when the competitor's right hand would be forward and is on the *port tack* when the competitor's left hand would be forward.

Zone The area around a *mark* within a distance of 30 metres. A kiteboard is in the *zone* when any part of her hull is in the *zone*.

Add the following definitions:

Capsized A kiteboard is *capsized* if
> (a) her kite is in the water, or
> (b) her lines are tangled with another kiteboard's lines.

Jumping A kiteboard is *jumping* when her hull, its appendages and the competitor are clear of the water.

Recovering
> (a) A kiteboard is *recovering* from the time she loses steerage way until she regains it, unless she is capsized.
> (b) A kiteboard is *recovering* from the time her kite is out of the water until she has steerage way.

F1 CHANGES TO THE RULES OF PART 1
[No changes.]

F2 CHANGES TO THE RULES OF PART 2

PART 2 – PREAMBLE
In the second sentence of the preamble, 'injury or serious damage' is changed to 'injury, serious damage or a tangle'.

13 WHILE TACKING
Rule 13 is deleted.

16 CHANGING COURSE OR KITE POSITION
Rule 16 is changed to:

16.1 When a right-of-way kiteboard changes course or the position of her kite, she shall give the other kiteboard *room* to continue *keeping clear*.

16.2 In addition, on a beat to windward when a *port-tack* kiteboard is *keeping clear* by sailing to pass to leeward of a *starboard-tack* kiteboard, the *starboard-tack* kiteboard shall not bear away or change the position of her kite if as a result the *port-tack* kiteboard must change course or the position of her kite immediately to continue *keeping clear*.

17 ON THE SAME TACK; PROPER COURSE
Rule 17 is deleted.

18 MARK-ROOM
Rule 18 is changed to:

18.1 When Rule 18 Applies

Rule 18 applies between kiteboards when they are required to leave a *mark* on the same side and at least one of them is in the *zone*. However, it does not apply

(a) between a kiteboard approaching a *mark* and one leaving it, or

(b) between kiteboards on opposite *tacks*.

Rule 18 no longer applies between kiteboards when *mark-room* has been given.

18.2 Giving Mark-Room

(a) When the first kiteboard reaches the *zone*,

    (1) if kiteboards are *overlapped*, the outside kiteboard at that moment shall thereafter give the inside kiteboard *mark-room*.

    (2) if kiteboards are not *overlapped*, the kiteboard that has not reached the *zone* shall thereafter give *mark-room*.

(b) If the kiteboard entitled to *mark-room* leaves the *zone*, the entitlement to *mark-room* ceases and rule 18.2(a) is applied again if required based on the relationship of the kiteboards at the time rule 18.2(a) is re-applied.

(c) If a kiteboard obtained an inside *overlap* and, from the time the *overlap* began, the outside kiteboard is unable to give *mark-room*, she is not required to give it.

18.3 Tacking and Gybing

When an inside *overlapped* right-of-way kiteboard must change *tack* at a *mark* to sail her *proper course*, until she changes *tack* she shall sail no farther from the *mark* than needed to sail that course. Rule 18.3 does not apply at a gate *mark* or a finishing *mark* and a kiteboard shall not be penalized for breaking this rule unless the course of another kiteboard was affected by the breach of this rule.

20 ROOM TO TACK AT AN OBSTRUCTION

Rule 20.1(a) is changed to:

(a) she is approaching an *obstruction*, and, to avoid it safely, will soon need to make a substantial change of her course or the position of her kite, and

Add new rule 20.5:

20.5 Arm Signals

The following arm signals are required in addition to the hails

(a) for *room* to tack, repeatedly and clearly circling one hand over the head; and

(b) for 'You tack', repeatedly and clearly pointing at the other kiteboard and waving the arm to windward.

Section D – Preamble

The preamble to Section D is changed to:

When rule 21 or 22 applies between two kiteboards, Section A and C rules do not.

21   STARTING ERRORS; TAKING PENALTIES; JUMPING

Rule 21.3 is changed and new rule 21.4 is added:

21.3   During the last minute before her starting signal, a kiteboard that stops, slows down significantly, or one that is not making significant forward progress shall *keep clear* of all others unless she is accidentally *capsized*.

21.4   A kiteboard that is *jumping* shall *keep clear* of one that is not.

22   CAPSIZED; RECOVERING; AGROUND; RESCUING

Rule 22 is changed to:

22.1   If possible, a kiteboard shall avoid a kiteboard that is *capsized*, is aground, or is trying to help a person or vessel in danger.

22.2   A kiteboard that is *recovering* shall *keep clear* of a kiteboard that is not.

F3   CHANGES TO THE RULES OF PART 3

26   STARTING RACES

Rule 26 is changed to:

Races shall be started by using the following signals. Times shall be taken from the visual signals; the absence of a sound signal shall be disregarded.

Minutes before starting signal	Visual signal	Sound signal	Means
3	Class flag	One	Warning signal
2	U or black flag	One	Preparatory signal
1	U or black flag removed	One long	One minute
0	Class flag removed	One	Starting signal

World Sailing Rules

29 RECALLS
Rule 29.1 is deleted.

30 STARTING PENALTIES
Rules 30.1 and 30.2 are deleted.

In rules 30.3 and 30.4, 'hull' is changed to 'hull or competitor'.

In rule 30.4, 'sail number' is changed to 'competitor number'.

31 TOUCHING A MARK
Rule 31 is changed to:
While *racing*, a kiteboard shall not touch a windward *mark*.

36 RACES RESTARTED OR RESAILED
Rule 36(b) is changed to:
(b) cause a kiteboard to be penalized except under rule 2, 30.2, 30.4 or 69 or under rule 14 when she has caused injury, serious damage or a tangle.

F4 CHANGES TO THE RULES OF PART 4

41 OUTSIDE HELP
Add new rules 41(e) and 41(f):
(e) help from another competitor in the same race to assist a relaunch;
(f) help to change equipment, but only in the launching area.

42 PROPULSION
Rule 42 is changed to:

42.1 Basic Rule
Except when permitted in rule 42.2, a kiteboard shall compete by using only the wind and water to increase, maintain or decrease her speed.

42.2 Exceptions
(a) A kiteboard may be propelled by unassisted actions of the competitor on the kiteboard.
(b) A competitor may swim, walk or paddle while *capsized* or *recovering*, provided that the kiteboard does not gain a significant advantage in the race.
(c) Any means of propulsion may be used to help a person or another vessel in danger.

43   EXONERATION

Rule 43.1(c) is changed to:

(c) A right-of-way kiteboard, or one sailing within the *room* or *mark-room* to which she is entitled, is exonerated for breaking rule 14 if the contact does not cause damage, injury or a tangle.

Add new rule 43.1(d):

(d) When a kiteboard breaks rule 15 and there is no contact, she is exonerated for her breach.

44   PENALTIES AT THE TIME OF AN INCIDENT

Rules 44.1 and 44.2 are changed to:

44.1 Taking a Penalty

A kiteboard may take a One-Turn Penalty when she may have broken one or more rules of Part 2 or rule 31 in an incident while *racing*. Alternatively, the notice of race or sailing instructions may specify the use of the Scoring Penalty or some other penalty, in which case the specified penalty shall replace the One-Turn Penalty. However,

(a) when a kiteboard may have broken a rule of Part 2 and rule 31 in the same incident she need not take the penalty for breaking rule 31; and

(b) if the kiteboard caused injury, damage or a tangle or, despite taking a penalty, gained a significant advantage or caused significant disadvantage to the other kiteboard in the race or series by her breach, her penalty shall be to retire.

44.2 One-Turn Penalty

After getting well clear of other kiteboards as soon after the incident as possible, a kiteboard takes a One-Turn Penalty by promptly making one turn with her hull appendage in the water. The turn shall include one completed tack and one completed gybe. When a kiteboard takes the penalty at or near the finishing line, her hull and competitor shall be completely on the course side of the line before she *finishes*.

PART 4 RULES DELETED

Rules 45, 48, 49, 50.2, 51, 52, 54, 55 and 56.1 are deleted.

F5   CHANGES TO THE RULES OF PART 5

61   PROTEST REQUIREMENTS

Rule 61.1(a) is changed to:

(a) The protesting kiteboard shall inform the other kiteboard at the first reasonable opportunity. When her *protest* will concern an incident in the racing area, she shall hail 'Protest' at the first reasonable opportunity. However,

(1) if the other kiteboard is beyond hailing distance, the protesting kiteboard need not hail but she shall inform the other kiteboard at the first reasonable opportunity;

(2) no red flag need be displayed;

(3) if the incident was an error by the other kiteboard in *sailing the course*, she need not hail but she shall inform the other kiteboard before that kiteboard *finishes* or at the first reasonable opportunity after she *finishes*;

(4) if at the time of the incident it is obvious to the protesting kiteboard that either competitior is in danger, or that injury, serious damage or a tangle resulted, the requirements of this rule do not apply to her, but she shall attempt to inform the other kiteboard within the time limit of rule 61.3.

63   HEARINGS

For a race of an elimination series that will qualify a kiteboard to compete in a later stage of an event, rules 61.2 and 65.2 are deleted and rule 63.6 is changed to:

63.6 *Protests* and requests for redress need not be in writing; they shall be made orally to a member of the protest committee as soon as reasonably possible following the race. The protest committee may take evidence in any way it considers appropriate and may communicate its decision orally.

64   DECISIONS

Add new rule 64.2(c):

(c) if a kiteboard has broken a *rule* and, as a result, caused a tangle for the second or subsequent time during the event, her penalty shall be a disqualification that is not excludable.

Rules 64.4(a) and 64.4(b) are changed to:

(a) When the protest committee finds that deviations in excess of acceptable manufacturing tolerances were caused by damage or normal wear and do not improve the performance of the kiteboard, it shall not penalize her. However, the kiteboard shall not *race* again until the deviations have been corrected, except when the protest committee decides there is or has been no reasonable opportunity to do so.

(b) When the protest committee is in doubt about any matter concerning the measurement of a kiteboard, the interpretation of a class rule, or a matter involving damage to a kiteboard, it shall refer its questions, together with the relevant facts, to an authority responsible for interpreting the rule. In making its decision, the committee shall be bound by the reply of the authority.

70 APPEALS AND REQUESTS TO A NATIONAL AUTHORITY
Add new rule 70.7:

70.7 Appeals are not permitted in disciplines and formats with elimination series.

F6 CHANGES TO THE RULES OF PART 6
[No changes.]

F7 CHANGES TO THE RULES OF PART 7

90 RACE COMMITTEE; SAILING INSTRUCTIONS; SCORING
The last sentence of rule 90.2(c) is changed to: 'Oral instructions may be given only if the procedure is stated in the sailing instructions.'

F8 CHANGES TO APPENDIX A

A1 NUMBER OF RACES; OVERALL SCORES
Rule A1 is changed to:
The number of races scheduled and the number required to be completed to constitute a series shall be stated in the notice of race or sailing instructions. If an event includes more than one discipline or format, the notice of race or sailing instructions shall state how the overall scores are to be calculated.

A5 SCORES DETERMINED BY THE RACE COMMITTEE
Rule A5.2 is changed to:

A5.2 A kiteboard that did not *start*, did not *sail the course*, did not *finish*, retired or was disqualified shall be scored points for the finishing place one more than the number of kiteboards entered in the series or, in a race of an elimination series, the number of kiteboards in that heat. A kiteboard that is penalized under rule 30.2 shall be scored points as provided in rule 44.3(c).

A10   SCORING ABBREVIATIONS

Add to Rule A10:

DCT   Disqualified after causing a tangle in an incident

F9   CHANGES TO APPENDIX G

Appendix G is changed to:

Appendix G – Identification

G1   Every kiteboard shall be identified as follows:

(a) Each competitor shall be provided with and wear a bib with a personal competition number of no more than three digits. The bib shall be worn as intended with the competition number clearly displayed.

(b) The numbers shall be displayed as high as possible on the front, back and sleeves of the bib. They should be at least 20 cm tall on the back and at least 6 cm tall on the front and the sleeves.

(c) The numbers shall be Arabic numerals, all of the same solid colour, clearly legible and in a commercially available typeface giving the same or better legibility as Helvetica. The colour of the numbers shall contrast with the colour of the bib.

APPENDIX G – IDENTIFICATION ON SAILS

See rule 77.

G1   WORLD CLASS BOATS

G1.1 Identification

Every boat of a World Sailing Class shall carry on her mainsail and, as provided in rule G1.3(c) for letters and numbers only, on her spinnaker and headsail

(a) the insignia denoting her class;

(b) at all international events, except when the boats are provided to all competitors, national letters denoting her national authority from the table below. For the purposes of this rule, international events are World Sailing events, world and continental championships, and events described as international events in their notices of race and sailing instructions; and

(c) a sail number of no more than four digits allotted by her national authority or, when so required by the class rules, by the class association. The four-digit limitation does not apply to classes whose World Sailing membership or recognition took effect before 1 April 1997. Alternatively, if permitted in the class rules, an owner may be allotted a personal sail number by the relevant issuing authority, which may be used on all his boats in that class.

Sails measured before 31 March 1999 shall comply with rule G1.1 or with the rules applicable at the time of measurement.

Note: An up-to-date version of the table below is available on the World Sailing website.

World Sailing Rules

NATIONAL SAIL LETTERS

National authority	Letters	National authority	Letters
Algeria	ALG	Czech Republic	CZE
American Samoa	ASA	Denmark	DEN
Andorra	AND	Djibouti	DJI
Angola	ANG	Dominican Republic	DOM
Antigua	ANT	Ecuador	ECU
Argentina	ARG	Egypt	EGY
Armenia	ARM	El Salvador	ESA
Aruba	ARU	Estonia	EST
Australia	AUS	Fiji	FIJ
Austria	AUT	Finland	FIN
Azerbaijan	AZE	France	FRA
Bahamas	BAH	Georgia	GEO
Bahrain	BRN	Germany	GER
Barbados	BAR	Great Britain	GBR
Belarus	BLR	Greece	GRE
Belgium	BEL	Grenada	GRN
Belize	BIZ	Guam	GUM
Bermuda	BER	Guatemala	GUA
Brazil	BRA	Hong Kong, China	HKG
Botswana	BOT	Hungary	HUN
British Virgin Islands	IVB	Iceland	ISL
Brunei Darussalam	BRU	India	IND
Bulgaria	BUL	Indonesia	INA
Cambodia	CAM	Iran	IRN
Canada	CAN	Iraq	IRQ
Cayman Islands	CAY	Ireland	IRL
Chile	CHI	Israel	ISR
China, PR	CHN	Italy	ITA
Chinese Taipei	TPE	Jamaica	JAM
Colombia	COL	Japan	JPN
Cook Islands	COK	Kazakhstan	KAZ
Croatia	CRO	Kenya	KEN
Cuba	CUB	Korea, DPR	PRK
Cyprus	CYP	Korea, Republic of	KOR

National authority	Letters	National authority	Letters
Kosovo	KOS	Philippines	PHI
Kuwait	KUW	Poland	POL
Kyrgyzstan	KGZ	Portugal	POR
Latvia	LAT	Puerto Rico	PUR
Lebanon	LIB	Qatar	QAT
Libya	LBA	Romania	ROU
Liechtenstein	LIE	Russia	RUS
Lithuania	LTU	Samoa	SAM
Luxembourg	LUX	San Marino	SMR
Macau, China	MAC	Senegal	SEN
Madagascar	MAD	Serbia	SRB
Malaysia	MAS	Seychelles	SEY
Malta	MLT	Singapore	SIN
Mauritius	MRI	Slovak Republic	SVK
Mexico	MEX	Slovenia	SLO
Moldova	MDA	South Africa	RSA
Monaco	MON	Spain	ESP
Montenegro	MNE	Sri Lanka	SRI
Montserrat	MNT	St Kitts & Nevis	SKN
Morocco	MAR	St Lucia	LCA
Mozambique	MOZ	Sudan	SUD
Myanmar	MYA	Sweden	SWE
Namibia	NAM	Switzerland	SUI
Netherlands	NED	Tahiti	TAH
Netherlands Antilles	AHO	Tanzania	TAN
New Zealand	NZL	Thailand	THA
Nigeria	NGR	Timore Leste	TLS
North Macedonia	MKD	Trinidad & Tobago	TTO
Norway	NOR	Tunisia	TUN
Oman	OMA	Turkey	TUR
Pakistan	PAK	Turks & Caicos	TKS
Palestine	PLE	Uganda	UGA
Panama	PAN	Ukraine	UKR
Papua New Guinea	PNG	United Arab Emirates	UAE
Paraguay	PAR	United States of America	USA
Peru	PER	Uruguay	URU

National authority	Letters	National authority	Letters
US Virgin Islands	ISV	Vietnam	VIE
Vanuatu	VAN	Zimbabwe	ZIM
Venezuela	VEN		

G1.2 Specification

(a) National letters and sail numbers shall be:
   (1) in capital letters and Arabic numerals,
   (2) of the same colour,
   (3) of a contrasting colour to the body of the sail, and
   (4) of a sans-serif typeface.

In addition, the letters and numbers identifying the boat shall be clearly legible when the sail is set.

(b) The height of characters and space between adjoining characters on the same and opposite sides of the sail shall be related to the boat's overall length as follows:

Overall length	Minimum height	Minimum space between characters and from edge of sail
Under 3.5 m	230 mm	45 mm
3.5 m – 8.5 m	300 mm	60 mm
8.5 m – 11 m	375 mm	75 mm
Over 11 m	450 mm	90 mm

G1.3 Positioning

Class insignia, national letters and sail numbers shall be positioned as follows:

(a) General
   (1) Class insignia, national letters and sail numbers, where applicable, shall be place on both sides and such that those on the starboard side are uppermost.
   (2) National letters shall be placed above the sail numbers on each side of the sail.

(b) Mainsails
   (1) The class insignia, national letters and sail numbers shall, if possible, be wholly above an arc whose centre is the head point and whose radius is 60% of the leech length.
   (2) The class insignia shall be placed above the national letters. If the class insignia is of a design that it may be placed back to back, then it may be so placed.

(c) Headsails and Spinnakers
(1) National letters and sail numbers are only required on a headsail whose foot length is greater than 1.3 x foretriangle base.
(2) The national letters and sail numbers of headsails shall be displayed wholly below an arc whose centre is the head point and whose radius is 50% of the luff length and, if possible, wholly above an arc whose radius is 75% of the luff length.
(3) The national letters and sail number shall be displayed on the front side of a spinnaker but may be placed on both sides. They shall be displayed wholly below an arc whose centre is the head point and whose radius is 40% of the foot median and, if possible, wholly above an arc whose radius is 60% of the foot median.

G2   OTHER BOATS

Other boats shall comply with the rules of their national authority or class association in regard to the allotment, carrying and size of insignia, letters and numbers. Such rules shall, when practicable, conform to the above requirements.

G3   CHARTERED OR LOANED BOATS

When so stated in the notice of race or sailing instructions, a boat chartered or loaned for an event may carry national letters or a sail number in contravention of her class rules.

G4   WARNINGS AND PENALTIES

When a protest committee finds that a boat has broken a rule of this appendix, it shall either warn her and give her time to comply or penalize her.

G5   CHANGES BY CLASS RULES

World Sailing Classes may change the rules of this appendix provided the changes have first been approved by World Sailing.

APPENDIX H – WEIGHING CLOTHING AND EQUIPMENT

See rule 50. This appendix shall not be changed by the notice of race, sailing instructions or prescriptions of national authorities.

H1 Items of clothing and equipment to be weighed shall be arranged on a rack. After being saturated in water the items shall be allowed to drain freely for one minute before being weighed. The rack must allow the items to hang as they would hang from clothes hangers, so as to allow the water to drain freely. Pockets that have drain-holes that cannot be closed shall be empty, but pockets or items that can hold water shall be full.

203 ✷

H2 When the weight recorded exceeds the amount permitted, the competitor may rearrange the items on the rack and the member of the technical committee in charge shall again soak and weigh them. This procedure may be repeated a second time if the weight still exceeds the amount permitted.

H3 A competitor wearing a dry suit may choose an alternative means of weighing the items.
(a) The dry suit and items of clothing and equipment that are worn outside the dry suit shall be weighed as described above.
(b) Clothing worn underneath the dry suit shall be weighed as worn while *racing*, without draining.
(c) The two weights shall be added together.

APPENDIX J – NOTICE OF RACE AND SAILING INSTRUCTIONS

See rules 89.2 and 90.2. In this appendix, the term 'event' includes a race or series of races.

A rule in the notice of race need not be repeated in the sailing instructions

Care should be taken to ensure that there is no conflict between rules in the notice of race, the sailing instructions or any other documentthat governs the event.

J1 NOTICE OF RACE CONTENTS

✱204

J1.1 The notice of race shall include the following:
(1) the title, place and dates of the event and name of the organizing authority;
(2) that the event will be governed by the *rules* as defined in *The Racing Rules of Sailing*;
(3) a list of any other documents that will govern the event (for example, *The Equipment Rules of Sailing*, to the extent that they apply), stating where or how each document or an electronic copy of it may be obtained;
(4) the classes to race, any handicap or rating system that will be used, and the classes to which it will apply; conditions of entry and any restrictions on entries;
(5) the procedures and times for registration or entry, including fees and any closing dates;
(6) the times of warning signals for the practice race, if one is scheduled, and the first race, and succeeding races if known.

J1.2 The notice of race shall include any of the following that will apply:
(1) times or procedures for equipment inspection or event measurement, or requirements for measurement or rating certificates;
(2) changes to the racing rules authorized by World Sailing under rule 86.2, referring specifically to each rule and stating the change (also include the statement from World Sailing authorizing the change);
(3) changes to class rules, as permitted under rule 87, referring specifically to each rule and stating the change;
(4) categorization or classification requirements that some or all competitors must satisfy;

(a) for sailor categorization (see rule 79 and the World Sailing Sailor Categorization Code), or

(b) for functional classification for Para World Sailing events (see World Sailing Para Classification Rules);

(5) that boats will be required to display advertising chosen and supplied by the organizing authority (see rule 6 and the World Sailing Advertising Code) and other information related to advertising;

(6) when entries from other countries are expected, any national prescriptions that may require advance preparation (see rule 88);

(7) prescriptions that will apply if boats will pass through the waters of more than one national authority while *racing*, and when they will apply (see rule 88.1);

(8) alternative communication required in place of hails under rule 20 (see rule 20.4(b));

(9) any change in the weight limit for a competitor's clothing and equipment permitted by rule 50.1(b);

(10) any requirements necessary for compliance with data protection legislation that applies in the venue of the event;

(11) an entry form, to be signed by the boat's owner or owner's representative, containing words such as 'I agree to be bound by *The Racing Rules of Sailing* and by all other *rules* that govern this event.';

(12) replacement of the rules of Part 2 with the right-of-way rules of the *International Regulations for Preventing Collisions at Sea* or other government right-of-way rules, the time(s) or place(s) they will apply, and any night signals to be used by the race committee.

J1.3 The notice of race shall include any of the following that will apply and that would help competitors decide whether to attend the event or that conveys other information they will need before the sailing instructions become available:

(1) changes to the racing rules permitted by rule 86, referring specifically to each rule and stating the change;

(2) changes to the national prescriptions (see rule 88.2);

(3) the time and place at which the sailing instructions will be available;

(4) a general description of the course, or type of courses, to be sailed;

(5) the scoring system, if different from the system in Appendix A, included by reference to class rules or other *rules* governing the event, or stated in full. State the number of races scheduled and the minimum number that must be

page

completed to constitute a series. If appropriate, for a series where the number of starters may vary substantially, state that rule A5.3 applies;

(6) the penalty for breaking a rule of Part 2, other than the Two-Turns Penalty;

(7) the time after which no warning signal will be made on the last scheduled day of racing;

(8) denial of the right of appeal, subject to rule 70.5;

(9) for chartered or loaned boats, whether rule G3 applies;

(10) prizes.

J2   SAILING INSTRUCTION CONTENTS

J2.1   Unless included in the notice of race, the sailing instructions shall include the following:

✴*204*

(1) the information in rules J1.3(1), (2) and (5) and, when applicable, rules J1.3(6), (7), (8), (9) and (10);;

(2) the schedule of races and the times of warning signals for each class;

(3) a complete description of the course(s) to be sailed, or a list of *marks* from which the course will be selected and, if relevant, how courses will be signalled;

(4) descriptions of *marks*, including starting and finishing *marks*, stating the order in which *marks* are to be passed and the side on which each is to be left and identifying all rounding *marks* (see the definition *Sail The Course*);

(5) descriptions of the starting and finishing lines, class flags and any special signals to be used;

(6) the race time limit, if any, for the first boat to *finish* (see rule 35);

(7) location(s) of official notice board(s) or address of online notice board; location of the race office.

J2.2   Unless included in the notice of race, the sailing instructions shall include those of the following that will apply:

(1) whether Appendix P will apply;

(2) when appropriate, at an event where entries from other countries are expected, a copy in English of the national prescriptions that will apply;

(3) procedure for changing the sailing instructions;

(4) procedure for giving oral changes to the sailing instructions on the water (see rule 90.2(c));

(5) safety requirements, such as requirements and signals for personal flotation devices, check-in at the starting area, and check-out and check-in ashore;

(6) signals to be made ashore and location of signal station(s);

(7) restrictions controlling changes to boats when supplied by the organizing authority;

(8) when and under what circumstances propulsion is permitted under rule 42.3(i);

(9) restrictions on use of support boats, plastic pools, radios, etc.; on trash disposal; on hauling out; and on outside assistance provided to a boat that is not *racing*;

(10) the racing area (a chart is recommended);

(11) location of the starting area and any restrictions on entering it;

(12) any special procedures or signals for individual or general recall;

(13) approximate course length and approximate length of windward legs;

(14) any special procedures or signals for changing a leg of the course (see rule 33);

(15) description of any object, area or line designated by the race committee to be an *obstruction* (see the definition *Obstruction*), and any restriction on entering such an area or crossing such a line;

(16) boats identifying *mark* locations;

(17) any special procedures for shortening the course or for *finishing* a shortened course;

(18) the time limit, if any, for boats other than the first boat to *finish* and any other time limits or target times that apply while boats are *racing*;

(19) declaration requirements;

(20) time allowances;

(21) time limits, place of hearings, and special procedures for *protests*, requests for redress or requests for reopening;

(22) the national authority's approval of the appointment of an international jury, when required under rule 91(b);

(23) the time limit for requesting a hearing under rule N1.4(b), if not 30 minutes;

(24) when required by rule 70.3, the national authority to which appeals and requests are required to be sent;

(25) substitution of competitors;

(26) the minimum number of boats appearing in the starting area required for a race to be started;

(27) when and where races *postponed* or *abandoned* for the day will be sailed;

(28) tides and currents;

(29) other commitments of the race committee and obligations of boats.

NOTICE OF RACE GUIDE
Previously Appendix K

SAILING INSTRUCTIONS GUIDE
Previously Appendix L

These guides, updated to conform to the rules in this edition of The Racing Rules of Sailing, *are available, in various formats, at the World Sailing website at* sailing.org/racingrules/documents. *National authorities are encouraged to translate the guides, and World Sailing will make translated versions available at that website.*

The guides, which will have a two-letter designation starting with 'K' or 'L', may be downloaded either as PDF documents or as Word documents. This will enable users to easily and quickly create, using the tested wording in the guides, either the notice of race or the sailing instructions, or both, for a particular event.

Suggestions for improving these guides are welcome and should be sent to rules@sailing.org.

APPENDIX M – RECOMMENDATIONS FOR PROTEST COMMITTEES

This appendix is advisory only; in some circumstances changing these procedures may be advisable. It is addressed primarily to protest committee chairmen but may also help judges, protest committee secretaries, race committees and others connected with protest and redress hearings.

In a protest or redress hearing, the protest committee should weigh all testimony with equal care; should recognize that honest testimony can vary, and even be in conflict, as a result of different observations and recollections; should resolve such differences as best it can; should recognize that no boat or competitor is guilty until a breach of a *rule* has been established to the satisfaction of the protest committee; and should keep an open mind until all the evidence has been heard as to whether a boat or competitor has broken a *rule*.

M1   PRELIMINARIES (may be performed by race office staff)
- Receive the protest or request for redress.
- Note on the form the time the *protest* or request is delivered and the *protest* time limit.
- Inform each *party*, and the race committee when necessary, when and where the hearing will be held.

M2   BEFORE THE HEARING

M2.1 Make sure that
- each *party* has a copy of or the opportunity to read the *protest* request for redress or allegation and has had reasonable time to prepare for the hearing.
- only one person from each boat (or *party*) is present unless an interpreter is needed.
- all boats and people involved are represented. If they are not, however, the committee may proceed under rule 63.3(b).
- boats' representatives were on board when required (rule 63.3(a)). When the *parties* were in different events, both organizing authorities must accept the composition of the protest committee (rule 63.8). In a *protest* concerning class rules, obtain the current class rules and identify the authority responsible for interpreting them (rule 64.4(b)).

M2.2 Determine if any members of the protest committee saw the incident. If so, require each of them to state that fact in the presence of the *parties* (rule 63.6(b)).

M2.3 Assess *conflicts of interest*

- Ensure that all protest committee members declare any possible *conflicts of interest*. At major events this will often be a formal written declaration made before the event starts that will be kept with the protest committee records.
- At the start of any hearing, ensure that the *parties* are aware of any *conflicts of interest* of protest committee members. Ask the *parties* if they consent to the members. If a *party* does not object as soon as possible after a *conflict of interest* has been declared, the protest committee may take this as consent to proceed and should record it.
- If a *party* objects to a member, the remainder of the protest committee members need to assess whether the *conflict of interest* is significant. The assessment will consider the level of the event, the level of the conflict and the perception of fairness. It may be acceptable to balance conflicts between protest committee members. Guidance may be found on the World Sailing website. Record the decision and the grounds for that decision.
- In cases of doubt it may be preferable to proceed with a smaller protest committee. Except for hearings under rule 69, there is no minimum number of protest committee members required.
- When a request for redress is made under rule 62.1(a) and is based on an improper action or omission of a body other than the protest committee, a member of that body should not be a member of the protest committee.

M3   THE HEARING

M3.1 Check the validity of the *protest* or request for redress.
- Are the contents adequate (rule 61.2 or 62)?
- Was it delivered in time? If not, is there good reason to extend the time limit (rule 61.3 or 62.2)?
- When required, was the protestor involved in or a witness to the incident (rule 60.1(a))?
- When necessary, was 'Protest' hailed and, if required, a red flag displayed correctly (rule 61.1(a))?
- When the flag or hail was not necessary, was the protestee informed?

- Decide whether the *protest* or request for redress is valid (rule 63.5).
- Once the validity of the *protest* or request has been determined, do not let the subject be introduced again unless truly new evidence is available.

M3.2 Take the evidence (rule 63.6).

- Ask the protestor and then the protestee to tell their stories. Then allow them to question one another. In a redress matter, ask the *party* to state the request.
- Make sure you know what facts each *party* is alleging before calling any witnesses. Their stories may be different.
- Allow anyone, including a boat's crew, to give evidence. It is the *party* who normally decides which witnesses to call, although the protest committee may also call witnesses (rule 63.6(a)). The question asked by a *party* 'Would you like to hear N?' is best answered by 'It is your choice.'
- Call each *party's* witnesses (and the protest committee's if any) one by one. Limit *parties* to questioning the witness(es) (they may wander into general statements).
- Invite the protestee to question the protestor's witness first (and vice versa). This prevents the protestor from leading his witness from the beginning.
- Allow members of the protest committee who saw the incident to give evidence (rule 63.6(b)), but only while the *parties* are present. Members who give evidence may be questioned, should take care to relate all they know about the incident that could affect the decision, and may remain on the protest committee (rule 63.3(a)).
- Try to prevent leading questions, but if that is impossible discount the evidence so obtained.
- The protest committee chairman should advise a *party* or a witness giving hearsay, repetitive or irrelevant evidence that the protest committee must give such evidence appropriate weight, which may be little or no weight at all.
- Accept written evidence from a witness who is not available to be questioned only if all *parties* agree. In doing so they forego their rights to question that witness (rule 63.6(c)).
- Ask one member of the committee to note down evidence, particularly times, distances, speeds, etc.
- Invite questions from protest committee members.
- Invite first the protestor and then the protestee to make a final statement of her case, particularly on any application or interpretation of the *rules*.

M3.3 Find the facts (rule 63.6(d)).
- Write down the facts; resolve doubts one way or the other.
- Call back *parties* for more questions if necessary.
- When appropriate, draw a diagram of the incident using the facts you have found.

M3.4 Decide the case (rule 64).
- Base the decision on the facts found (if you cannot, find some more facts).
- In redress cases, make sure that no further evidence is needed from boats that will be affected by the decision.

M3.5 Inform the *parties* (rule 65).
- Recall the *parties* and read them the facts found, conclusions and *rules* that apply, and the decision. When time presses it is permissible to read the decision and give the details later.
- Give any *party* a copy of the decision on request. File the *protest* or request for redress with the committee records.

M4 REOPENING A HEARING (rule 66)

M4.1 When a *party*, within the time limit, has asked for a hearing to be reopened, hear the *party* making the request, look at any video, etc., and decide whether there is any significant new evidence that might lead you to change your decision. Decide whether your interpretation of the *rules* may have been wrong; be open-minded as to whether you have made a mistake. If none of these applies refuse to reopen; otherwise schedule a hearing.

M4.2 Evidence is 'new'
- if it was not reasonably possible for the *party* asking for the reopening to have discovered the evidence before the original hearing,
- if the protest committee is satisfied that before the original hearing the evidence was diligently but unsuccessfully sought by the *party* asking for the reopening, or
- if the protest committee learns from any source that the evidence was not available to the *parties* at the time of the original hearing.

M5 GROSS MISCONDUCT (rule 69)

M5.1 An action under this rule is not a *protest*, but the protest committee gives its allegations in writing to the competitor before the hearing. The hearing is conducted under rules similar to those governing a protest hearing but the protest committee must have at least three members (rule 69.2(a)). Use the greatest care to protect the competitor's rights.

M5.2 A competitor or a boat cannot protest under rule 69, but the hearing request form of a competitor who tries to do so may be accepted as a report to the protest committee, which can then decide whether or not to call a hearing.

M5.3 Unless World Sailing has appointed a person for the role, the protest committee may appoint a person to present the allegation. This person might be a race official, the person making the allegation or other appropriate person. When no reasonable alternative person is available, a person who was appointed as a member of the protest committee may present the allegation.

M5.4 When it is desirable to call a hearing under rule 69 as a result of a Part 2 incident, it is important to hear any boat-vs.-boat *protest* in the normal way, deciding which boat, if any, broke which *rule*, before proceeding against the competitor under rule 69.

M5.5 Although action under rule 69 is taken against a competitor, boat owner or *support person*, and not a boat, a boat may also be penalized (rules 69.2(h)(2) and 64.5).

M5.6 When a protest committee upholds a rule 69 allegation it will need to consider if it is appropriate to report to either a national authority or World Sailing. Guidance on when to report may be found in the World Sailing Case Book. When the protest committee does make a report it may recommend whether or not further action should be taken.

M5.7 Unless the right of appeal is denied in accordance with rule 70.5, a *party* to a rule 69 hearing may appeal the decision of the protest committee.

M5.8 Further guidance for protest committees about misconduct may be found on the World Sailing website.

M6   APPEALS (rule 70 and Appendix R)
When decisions can be appealed,
- retain the papers relevant to the hearing so that the information can easily be used for an appeal. Is there a diagram endorsed or prepared by the protest committee? Are the facts found sufficient? (Example: Was there an *overlap*? Yes or No. 'Perhaps' is not a fact found.) Are the names of the protest committee members and other important information on the form?
- comments by the protest committee on any appeal should enable the appeals committee to picture the whole incident clearly; the appeals committee knows nothing about the situation.

M7   PHOTOGRAPHIC EVIDENCE

Photographs and videos can sometimes provide useful evidence but protest committees should recognize their limitations and note the following points:

- The *party* producing the photographic evidence is responsible for arranging the viewing.
- View the video several times to extract all the information from it.
- The depth perception of any single-lens camera is very poor; with a telephoto lens it is non-existent. When the camera views two *overlapped* boats at right angles to their course, it is impossible to assess the distance between them. When the camera views them head on, it is impossible to see whether an *overlap* exists unless it is substantial.
- Ask the following questions:
  - Where was the camera in relation to the boats?
  - Was the camera's platform moving? If so in what direction and how fast?
  - Is the angle changing as the boats approach the critical point? Fast panning causes radical change.
  - Did the camera have an unrestricted view throughout?

APPENDIX N – INTERNATIONAL JURIES

See rules 70.5 and 91(b). This appendix shall not be changed by the notice of race, sailing instructions or national prescriptions.

N1   COMPOSITION, APPOINTMENT AND ORGANIZATION

N1.1 An international jury shall be composed of experienced sailors with excellent knowledge of the racing rules and extensive protest committee experience. It shall be independent of and have no members from the race committee or the technical committee, and it shall be appointed by the organizing authority, subject to approval by the national authority if required (see rule 91(b)), or by World Sailing under rule 89.2(c).

N1.2 The jury shall consist of a chairman, a vice chairman if desired, and other members for a total of at least five. A majority shall be International Judges.

N1.3 No more than two members (three, in Groups M, N and Q) shall be from the same national authority.

N1.4 (a) The chairman of a jury may appoint one or more panels composed in compliance with rules N1.1, N1.2 and N1.3. This can be done even if the full jury is not composed in compliance with these rules.

(b) The chairman of a jury may appoint panels of at least three members each, of which the majority shall be International Judges. Members of each panel shall be from at least three different national authorities except in Groups M, N and Q, where they shall be from at least two different national authorities. If dissatisfied with a panel's decision, a *party* is entitled to a hearing by a panel composed in compliance with rules N1.1, N1.2 and N1.3, except concerning the facts found, if requested within 30 minutes or the time limit specified in the sailing instructions.

N1.5 When a full jury, or a panel, has fewer than five members, because of illness or emergency, and no qualified replacements are available, it remains properly constituted if it consists of at least three members and if at least two of them are International Judges. When there are three or four members they shall be from at least three different national authorities except in Groups M, N and Q, where they shall be from at least two different national authorities.

N1.6 When it is considered desirable that some members not participate in discussing and deciding a *protest* or request for redress, and no qualified replacements are available, the jury or panel remains properly constituted if at least three members remain and at least two of them are International Judges.

N1.7 In exception to rules N1.1 and N1.2, World Sailing may in limited circumstances (see World Sailing Regulation 25.8.13) authorize an international jury consisting of a total of only three members. All members shall be International Judges. The members shall be from three different national authorities (two, in Groups M, N and Q). The authorization shall be stated in a letter of approval to the organizing authority and in the notice of race or sailing instructions, and the letter shall be posted on the official notice board.

N1.8 When the national authority's approval is required for the appointment of an international jury (see rule 91(b)), notice of its approval shall be included in the sailing instructions or be posted on the official notice board.

N1.9 If the jury or a panel acts while not properly constituted, its decisions may be appealed.

N2 RESPONSIBILITIES

N2.1 An international jury is responsible for hearing and deciding all *protests*, requests for redress and other matters arising under the rules of Part 5. When asked by the organizing authority, the race committee or the technical committee, it shall advise and assist them on any matter directly affecting the fairness of the competition.

N2.2 Unless the organizing authority directs otherwise, the jury shall decide
(a) questions of eligibility, measurement or rating certificates; and
(b) whether to authorize the substitution of competitors, boats or equipment when a *rule* requires such a decision.

N2.3 The jury shall also decide matters referred to it by the organizing authority, the race committee or the technical committee.

N3 PROCEDURES

N3.1 Members shall not be regarded as having a significant *conflict of interest* (see rule 63.4) by reason of their nationality, club membership or similar. When otherwise considering a significant *conflict of interest* as required by rule 63.4, considerable weight must be given to the fact that decisions of an international jury cannot be appealed and this may affect the perception of fairness and lower the level of conflict that is significant. In case of doubt, the hearing should proceed as permitted by rule N1.6.

N3.2 If a panel fails to agree on a decision it may adjourn, in which case the chairman shall refer the matter to a properly constituted panel with as many members as possible, which may be the full jury.

N4 MISCONDUCT (Rule 69)

N4.1 The World Sailing Disciplinary Code, contains procedures that apply to specific international events with regard to the appointment of a person to conduct any investigation. These procedures override any conflicting provision of this appendix.

N4.2 A person shall be responsible for presenting to the hearing panel any allegations of misconduct under rule 69. This person shall not be a member of the hearing panel but may be a member of the jury. Such a person shall be required to make full disclosure of all material that may come into his possession in the course of his investigation to the person subject to allegations of a breach of rule 69.

N4.3 Prior to a hearing, the hearing panel, to the extent practically possible, shall not act as an investigator of any allegations made under rule 69. However, during the hearing the panel shall be entitled to ask any investigative questions it may see fit.

N4.4 If the panel decides to call a hearing, all material disclosed to the panel in order for them to make that decision must be disclosed to the person subject to the allegations before the hearing begins.

APPENDIX P – SPECIAL PROCEDURES FOR RULE 42

All or part of this appendix applies only if the notice of race or sailing instructions so state.

P1 OBSERVERS AND PROCEDURE

P1.1 The protest committee may appoint observers, including protest committee members, to act in accordance with rule P1.2. A person with a significant *conflict of interest* shall not be appointed as an observer.

P1.2 An observer appointed under rule P1.1 who sees a boat breaking rule 42 may penalize her by, as soon as reasonably possible, making a sound signal, pointing a yellow flag at her and hailing her sail number, even if she is no longer *racing*. A boat so penalized shall not be penalized a second time under rule 42 for the same incident.

P2 PENALTIES

P2.1 First Penalty
When a boat is first penalized under rule P1.2 her penalty shall be a Two-Turns Penalty under rule 44.2. If she fails to take it she shall be disqualified without a hearing.

P2.2 Second Penalty
When a boat is penalized a second time during the event, she shall promptly retire from the race. If she fails to do so she shall be disqualified without a hearing and her score shall not be excluded.

P2.3 Third and Subsequent Penalties
When a boat is penalized a third or subsequent time during the event, she shall promptly retire. If she does so her penalty shall be disqualification without a hearing and her score shall not be excluded. If she fails to do so her penalty shall be disqualification without a hearing from all races in the event, with no score excluded, and the protest committee shall consider calling a hearing under rule 69.2.

P2.4 Penalties Near the Finishing Line
If a boat is penalized under rule P2.2 or P2.3 and it was not reasonably possible for her to retire before *finishing*, she shall be scored as if she had retired promptly.

P3   POSTPONEMENT, GENERAL RECALL OR ABANDONMENT

If a boat has been penalized under rule P1.2 and the race committee signals a *postponement*, general recall or *abandonment*, the penalty is cancelled, but it is still counted to determine the number of times she has been penalized during the event.

P4   REDRESS LIMITATION

A boat shall not be given redress for an action by a member of the protest committee or its designated observer under rule P1.2 unless the action was improper due to a failure to take into account a race committee signal or a class rule.

P5   FLAGS O AND R

P5.1 When Rule P5 Applies

Rule P5 applies if the class rules permit pumping, rocking and ooching when the wind speed exceeds a specified limit.

P5.2 Before the Starting Signal

(a) The race committee may signal that pumping, rocking and ooching are permitted, as specified in the class rules, by displaying flag O before or with the warning signal.

(b) If the wind speed becomes less than the specified limit after flag O has been displayed, the race committee may *postpone* the race. Then, before or with a new warning signal, the committee shall display either flag R, to signal that rule 42 as changed by the class rules applies, or flag O, as provided in rule P5.2(a).

(c) If flag O or flag R is displayed before or with the warning signal, it shall be displayed until the starting signal.

P5.3 After the Starting Signal

After the starting signal,

(a) if the wind speed exceeds the specified limit, the race committee may display flag O with repetitive sounds at a *mark* to signal that pumping, rocking and ooching are permitted, as specified in the class rules, after passing the *mark*;

(b) if flag O has been displayed and the wind speed becomes less than the specified limit, the race committee may display flag R with repetitive sounds at a *mark* to signal that rule 42, as changed by the class rules, applies after passing the *mark*.

APPENDIX R – PROCEDURES FOR APPEALS AND REQUESTS

See rule 70. A national authority may change this appendix by prescription but it shall not be changed by notice of race or sailing instructions.

R1   APPEALS AND REQUESTS

Appeals, requests by protest committees for confirmation or correction of their decisions, and requests for interpretations of the *rules* shall be made in compliance with this appendix.

R2   SUBMISSION OF DOCUMENTS

R2.1 To make an appeal,

(a) no later than 15 days after receiving the protest committee's written decision or its decision not to reopen a hearing, the appellant shall send an appeal and a copy of the protest committee's decision to the national authority. The appeal shall state why the appellant believes the protest committee's decision or its procedures were incorrect;

(b) when the hearing required by rule 63.1 has not been held within 30 days after a *protest* or request for redress was delivered, the appellant shall, within a further 15 days, send an appeal with a copy of the *protest* or request and any relevant correspondence. The national authority shall extend the time if there is good reason to do so;

(c) when the protest committee fails to comply with rule 65, the appellant shall, within a reasonable time after the hearing, send an appeal with a copy of the *protest* or request and any relevant correspondence.

If a copy of the *protest* or request is not available, the appellant shall instead send a statement of its substance.

R2.2 The appellant shall also send, with the appeal or as soon as possible thereafter, all of the following documents that are available to her:

(a) the written *protest*(s) or request(s) for redress;

(b) a diagram, prepared or endorsed by the protest committee, showing the positions and tracks of all boats involved, the course to the next *mark* and the required side, the force and direction of the wind, and, if relevant, the depth of water and direction and speed of any current;

(c) the notice of race, the sailing instructions, any other documents governing the event, and any changes to them;

(d) any additional relevant documents; and

(e) the names, postal and email addresses, and telephone numbers of all *parties* to the hearing and the protest committee chairman.

R2.3 A request from a protest committee for confirmation or correction of its decision shall be sent no later than 15 days after the decision and shall include the decision and the documents listed in rule R2.2. A request for an interpretation of the *rules* shall include assumed facts.

R3 **RESPONSIBILITIES OF NATIONAL AUTHORITY AND PROTEST COMMITTEE**

Upon receipt of an appeal or a request for confirmation or correction, the national authority shall send to the *parties* and protest committee copies of the appeal or request and the protest committee's decision. It shall ask the protest committee for any relevant documents listed in rule R2.2 not sent by the appellant or the protest committee, and the protest committee shall promptly send them to the national authority. When the national authority has received them it shall send copies to the *parties*.

R4 **COMMENTS AND CLARIFICATIONS**

R4.1 The *parties* and protest committee may make comments on the appeal or request or on any of the documents listed in rule R2.2 by sending them in writing to the national authority.

R4.2 The national authority may seek clarifications of *rules* governing the event from organizations that are not *parties* to the hearing.

R4.3 The national authority shall send copies of comments and clarifications received to the *parties* and protest committee as appropriate.

R4.4 Comments on any document shall be made no later than 15 days after receiving it from the national authority.

R5 **INADEQUATE FACTS; REOPENING**

The national authority shall accept the protest committee's finding of facts except when it decides they are inadequate. In that case it shall require the committee to provide additional facts or other information, or to reopen the hearing and report any new finding of facts, and the committee shall promptly do so.

R6   WITHDRAWING AN APPEAL

An appellant may withdraw an appeal before it is decided by accepting the protest committee's decision.

APPENDIX S – STANDARD SAILING INSTRUCTIONS

This appendix applies only if the notice of race so states.

These Standard Sailing Instructions may be used at an event in place of printed sailing instructions made available to each boat. To use them, state in the notice of race that 'The sailing instructions will consist of the instructions in RRS Appendix S, Standard Sailing Instructions, and supplementary sailing instructions that will be posted on the official notice board located at _____.'

The supplementary sailing instructions will include:
1. *The location of the race office and of the flag pole on which signals made ashore will be displayed (see SI 4.1 below).*
2. *A table showing the schedule of races, including the day and date of each scheduled day of racing, the number of races scheduled each day, the scheduled time of the first warning signal each day, and the latest time for a warning signal on the last scheduled day of racing.*
3. *A list of the marks that will be used and a description of each one (SI 8). How new marks will differ from original marks (SI 10).*
4. *The time limits, if any, that are listed in SI 12.*
5. *Any changes or additions to the instructions in this appendix.*

A copy of the supplementary sailing instructions will be available to competitors on request.

SAILING INSTRUCTIONS

1   RULES

1.1   The event will be governed by the rules as defined in *The Racing Rules of Sailing.*

2   NOTICES TO COMPETITORS

2.1   Notices to competitors will be posted on the official notice board.

2.2   Supplementary sailing instructions (called 'the supplement' below) will be posted on the official notice board.

3 CHANGES TO SAILING INSTRUCTIONS

3.1 Any change to the sailing instructions will be posted before 0800 on the day it will take effect, unless this time is changed in the supplement. Any change to the schedule of races will be posted by 2000 on the day before it will take effect.

4 SIGNALS MADE ASHORE

4.1 Signals made ashore will be displayed from the flag pole. The supplement will state its location.

5 SCHEDULE OF RACES

5.1 The supplement will include a table showing the days, dates, number of races scheduled, the scheduled times of the first warning signal each day, and the latest time for a warning signal on the last scheduled day of racing.

5.2 To alert boats that a race or sequence of races will begin soon, the orange starting line flag will be displayed with one sound at least five minutes before a warning signal is made.

6 CLASS FLAGS

6.1 Each class flag will be the class insignia on a plain background or as stated in the supplement.

7 THE COURSES

7.1 No later than the warning signal, the race committee will designate the course, and it may also display the approximate compass bearing of the first leg.

7.2 The course diagrams are on the pages following SI 13. They show the courses, the order in which marks are to be passed, and the side on which each mark is to be left. The supplement may include additional courses.

8 MARKS

8.1 A list of the marks that will be used, including a description of each one, will be included in the supplement.

9 THE START

9.1 Races will be started by using RRS 26.

9.2 The starting line will be between a staff displaying an orange flag on the race committee vessel and the course side of the starting mark.

10 CHANGE OF THE NEXT LEG OF THE COURSE

10.1 To change the next leg of the course, the race committee will lay a new mark (or move the finishing line) and remove the original mark as soon as practicable. When in a subsequent change a new mark is replaced, it will be replaced by an original mark.

11 THE FINISH

11.1 The finishing line will be between a staff displaying a blue flag on the race committee vessel and the course side of the finishing mark.

12 TIME LIMITS

12.1 The supplement will state which of the following time limits, if any, will apply and, for each, the time limit.
   • Mark 1 Time Limit Time limit for the first boat to pass Mark 1.
   • Race Time Limit   Time limit for the first boat to start, sail the course and finish.
   • Finishing Window   Time limit for boats to finish after the first boat starts, sails the course and finishes.

12.2 If no boat has passed Mark 1 within the Mark 1 Time Limit, the race shall be abandoned.

12.3 Boats failing to finish within the Finishing Window shall be scored Did Not Finish without a hearing. This changes RRS 35, A5.1 and A5.2.

13 PROTESTS AND REQUESTS FOR REDRESS

13.1 Hearing request forms are available at the race office. Protests and requests for redress or reopening shall be delivered there within the appropriate time limit.

13.2 For each class, the protest time limit is 60 minutes after the last boat has finished the last race of the day or the race committee signals no more racing today, which ever is later.

13.3 Notices will be posted no later than 30 minutes after the protest time limit to inform competitors of hearings in which they are parties or named as witnesses and where the hearings will be held.

13.4 Notices of protests by the race committee, technical committee or protest committee will be posted to inform boats under RRS 61.1(b).

13.5 On the last scheduled day of racing a request for redress based on a protest committee decision shall be delivered no later than 30 minutes after the decision was posted. This changes RRS 62.2.

COURSE DIAGRAMS

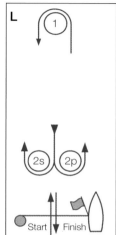

Course L – Windward/Leeward, Leeward Finish	
Signal	*Mark Rounding Order*
L2	Start – 1 – 2s/2p – 1 – Finish
L3	Start – 1 – 2s/2p – 1 – 2s/2p – 1 – Finish
L4	Start – 1 – 2s/2p – 1 – 2s/2p – 1 – 2s/2p – 1 – Finish

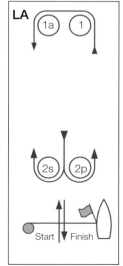

Course LA – Windward/Leeward with Offset Mark, Leeward Finish	
Signal	*Mark Rounding Order*
LA2	Start – 1 – 1a – 2s/2p – 1 – 1a – Finish
LA3	Start – 1 – 1a – 2s/2p – 1 – 1a – 2s/2p – 1 – 1a – Finish
LA4	Start – 1 – 1a – 2s/2p – 1 – 1a – 2s/2p – 1 – 1a – 2s/2p – 1 – 1a – Finish

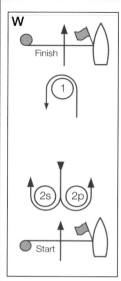

Course W – Windward/Leeward, Windward Finish	
Signal	Mark Rounding Order
W2	Start – 1 – 2s/2p – Finish
W3	Start – 1 – 2s/2p – 1 – 2s/2p – Finish
W4	Start – 1 – 2s/2p – 1 – 2s/2p – 1 – 2s/2p – Finish

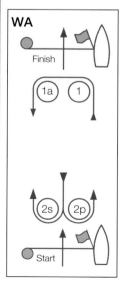

Course WA – Windward/Leeward with Offset Mark, Windward Finish	
Signal	Mark Rounding Order
WA2	Start – 1 – 1a – 2s/2p – Finish
WA3	Start – 1 – 1a – 2s/2p – 1 – 1a – 2s/2p – Finish
WA4	Start – 1 – 1a – 2s/2p – 1 – 1a – 2s/2p – 1 – 1a – 2s/2p – Finish

TL

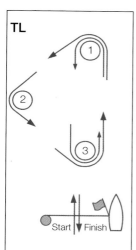

Course TL – Triangle, Leeward Finish	
Signal	*Mark Rounding Order*
TL2	Start – 1 – 2 – 3 – 1 – Finish
TL3	Start – 1 – 2 – 3 – 1 – 3 – 1 – Finish
TL4	Start – 1 – 2 – 3 – 1 – 3 – 1 – 3 – 1 – Finish

TW

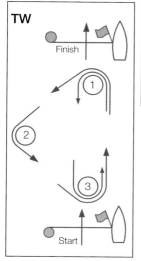

Course TW – Triangle, Windward Finish	
Signal	*Mark Rounding Order*
TW2	Start – 1 – 2 – 3 – Finish
TW3	Start – 1 – 2 – 3 – 1 – 3 – Finish
TW4	Start – 1 – 2 – 3 – 1 – 3 – 1 – 3 – Finish

APPENDIX T – ARBITRATION

This appendix applies only if the notice of race or sailing instructions so state.

Arbitration adds an extra step to the protest resolution process but can eliminate the need for some protest hearings, thus speeding up the process for events in which many protests are expected. Arbitration may not be appropriate for all events as it requires an additional knowledgeable person to act as the arbitrator. Further guidance on arbitration can be found in the World Sailing Judges Manual*, which can be downloaded from the World Sailing website.*

T1   POST-RACE PENALTIES

(a) Provided that rule 44.1(b) does not apply, a boat that may have broken one or more rules of Part 2 or rule 31 in an incident may take a Post-Race Penalty at any time after the race until the beginning of a protest hearing involving the incident.

(b) A Post-Race Penalty is a 30% Scoring Penalty calculated as stated in rule 44.3(c). However, rule 44.1(a) applies.

(c) A boat takes a Post-Race Penalty by delivering to the arbitrator or a member of the protest committee a written statement that she accepts the penalty and that identifies the race number and where and when the incident occurred.

T2   ARBITRATION MEETING

An arbitration meeting will be held prior to a protest hearing for each incident resulting in a *protest* by a boat involving one or more rules of Part 2 or rule 31, but only if each *party* is represented by a person who was on board at the time of the incident. No witnesses will be permitted. However, if the arbitrator decides that rule 44.1(b) may apply or that arbitration is not appropriate, the meeting will not be held, and if a meeting is in progress, it will be closed.

T3   ARBITRATOR'S OPINION

Based on the evidence given by the representatives, the arbitrator will offer an opinion as to what the protest committee is likely to decide:

(a) the *protest* is invalid,

(b) no boat will be penalized for breaking a *rule*, or

(c) one or more boats will be penalized for breaking a *rule*, identifying the boats and the penalties.

T4 ARBITRATION MEETING OUTCOMES

After the arbitrator offers an opinion,

(a) a boat may take a Post-Race Penalty, and

(b) a boat may ask to withdraw her *protest*. The arbitrator may then act on behalf of the protest committee in accordance with rule 63.1 to allow the withdrawal.

Unless all *protests* involving the incident are withdrawn, a protest hearing will be held.

EXPLANATORY SECTION

(Red marginal page references)

Definitions

**Clear Astern and Clear
Ahead; Overlap**

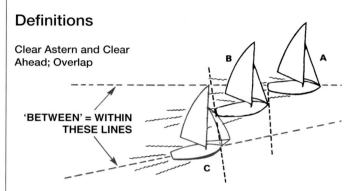

'BETWEEN' = WITHIN
THESE LINES

Watch out because a foresail, a spinnaker or a boomed-out jib could establish an overlap. The so-called 'transom line' is the critical overlap limit, but remember that it passes through the aftermost point of everything.

Boat B is 'between' A and C for the purpose of the definition, so C overlaps A if C overlaps B and B overlaps A. If boat B had been overlapping boat C and boat A, but on the far side of boat A, she would not have been a boat 'between' under this definition.

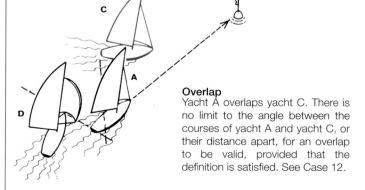

Overlap
Yacht A overlaps yacht C. There is no limit to the angle between the courses of yacht A and yacht C, or their distance apart, for an overlap to be valid, provided that the definition is satisfied. See Case 12.

222✱

Clear Astern and Clear Ahead; Overlap
Red has not established an overlap because her spinnaker is not in the normal position.

Overlap and Keep Clear
In this case, the definition says the boats are overlapped because they are sailing more than 90° from the true wind. However they are on opposite tacks so Rule 10 applies. Red must keep clear i.e. allow Black to sail her course (definition Keep Clear (a)) AND give Black 'wriggle room' i.e. keep a distance so Black can change course without immediate contact (definition Keep Clear (b)). The fact that under the definition they are overlapped allows them to anticipate the situation when they get to the zone of the mark. See below.

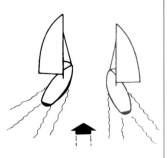

Overlap
Now the boats are overlapped because they are inside the zone and not on a beat to windward and Rule 18 applies. Black is now entitled to mark-room. Red cannot argue that this is a new overlap that Black obtained at the zone. Under the definition they have been overlapped for a long time so there is no doubt that Black is entitled to room.

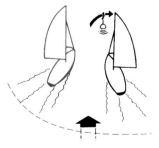

page

179 *189*

Fetching
See explanations under Rule 18.3 and 20.1.

Finishing and Racing
Even though the Red boat has received her winning gun, she would be disqualified for infringing Black or breaking rule 28.2 or 31, because she has not cleared the finishing line and is still racing. See also the preamble of Part 2. However she can only be DSQ by the Protest Committee after a valid protest. See Case 128.

211

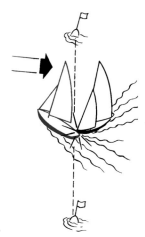

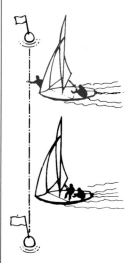

Finishing
The Red boat has not yet finished because no part of her hull has crossed the line. The position of the crew is not relevant. According to the dictionary, a bowsprit, retractable or permanent, is not a part of the hull.

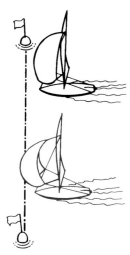

Finishing
Red has not yet finished because no part of her hull has crossed the line. The spinnaker and whether it is in normal position or not is not relevant. See also Rule 31.2 for what happens when a boat touches a finishing mark. A further point to mention is that a race committee is not allowed to override the definition of finishing. See Cases 45 and 82.

211

page

Keep Clear

A keep-clear boat does not break a rule when touched by a right-of-way boat's equipment that unforeseen suddenly moves out of its normal position. See Case 77.

✸*211*

However, a keep-clear boat must keep clear of another boat's equipment that is out of its normal position when possible because the equipment has been out of position long enough to be seen. See Case 91.

✸*212*

Keep Clear; On the same tack

Red is overtaking. Black has right of way according to Rule 11. Normally Red would be keeping clear, if Black could sail her course, and Black could not change course without giving Red room to keep clear according to Rule 16. But as they are overlapped the definition (Keep Clear (b)) says that Red must keep a distance to Black ('wriggle room') that allows her not only to keep her course, but also allows room for Black to change course without immediately making contact. Thus Black has a possibility to luff to protect her wind and avoid being overtaken. She must however comply with Rule 16 if she luffs. See also Case 60.

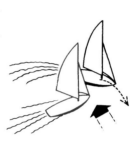

✸*220*

Leeward and Windward; Tack, Starboard or Port

Note that a boat is always on a tack, either starboard or port.

Tacking is not defined in the rules but is used in the common meaning of the word for the manoeuvre of changing tacks by passing head to wind. See also Rule 13.

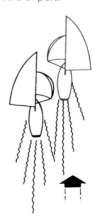

✸*158*

Gybing means changing the mainsail from one side to the other with the wind from behind. When a boat tacks or gybes it changes momentarily from one tack to another.

Leeward and Windward

Because these boats are on opposite tacks even if they overlap under the definition of overlap, neither complies with the definition of windward boat or leeward boat.

Leeward and Windward

Here neither boat is clear astern so the boats overlap. Black is on Red's leeward side so Black is the leeward boat and Red is the windward boat.

169 ✹

212 ✹

Mark-Room

See explanations under Rule 18. See also Case 144.

Obstruction

A change of course is only substantial when a boat would lose a substantial amount of ground by altering course. A small fishing buoy, for example, would not cause any obstruction because it would just slide along the side of the boat without stopping it. But a small object such as a post or a buoy and objects such as heavy seaweed, floating plastic or timber could be an obstruction for the purpose of Rule 20 (Room to Tack at an Obstruction). A racing boat can also be an obstruction but not a

212 ✹ continuing obstruction. See Case 41.

Proper Course

The proper course is not necessarily the shortest course: there can be more than one 'proper course'. The criteria for a proper course is that the boat should have a valid reason for steering that course and apply it with some consistency. The end result has nothing to do with it.

212 ✹ See Case 14.

Here, Black can bear away to sail the curved course to avoid the wind shade from the shore. See also Case 46.

Proper Course also depends on the existing conditions.

212 ✹ See Case 134

Room

The phrase 'seamanlike way' in the definition Room refers to the boat handling that can reasonably be expected from a competent, but not expert, crew of the appropriate number for the boat. So a boat cannot claim more room because her crew is small in number or inexperienced. See Cases 103 and 146.

❋*213*

Sail the Course

❋*196*

See explanations under Rule 28.1.

Rules

The rules included in the definition apply whether or not the NoR or SI so state, except the prescriptions of a national authority and appendix A Scoring which only apply when so stated in NoR or SI. See Case 98.

❋*213*

Starting

This boat has not crossed the line to start because no part of the hull has crossed. The position of the crew is not relevant.

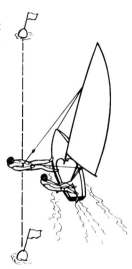

SPORTSMANSHIP

Sportsmanship is not a rule that you can violate, it is part of the fundamental principles of the sport of sailing; however if you commit a gross breach of a rule, of good manners, or of sportsmanship, the protest committee may call a hearing under Rule 69, or Rule 2 (Fair Sailing).

The Racing Rules have no direct way of preventing a competitor who has broken the Rules from continuing. But if you continue when you

213●

are sure you have broken a rule, and for example interfere with another competitor and force him to get a bad placing, you may be commiting a gross breach of sportsmanship. See Case 65.

232●

If you really have doubts as to who was right in an incident then you should protest. One or both boats could have been wrong and it is best to resolve the issue so that you know what is right next time. See Cases 1 and 68.

PART 1 – FUNDAMENTAL RULES

1.1 Helping Those In Danger

214●

Great importance is attached to racing sailors helping those in danger. Do not think that somebody else will look after the distressed vessel or person – you must attend any incident unless you are completely sure your presence is no longer required. See Case 20.

You must, of course, also help your own crew when in danger, but this is not a reason for seeking redress under Rule 62.

1.2 Life-Saving Equipment and Personal Flotation Devices

Note also that according to Rule 40 neither wet nor dry suits are acceptable as personal flotation devices.

2 Fair Sailing

*235/
214*●

Note that this rule also applies when **not** racing; a crew might deliberately damage a boat between races during a series. You can be disqualified between races, or you could be disqualified for a whole series. Cases 34, 47, 65, 73, 74 and 78 contain further interpretations of this rule.

3 Decision to Race

The responsibility of whether or not a boat races must rest finally with the boat and her crew. The organizers cannot be blamed or held responsible for not abandoning a race because of bad weather.

4 Acceptance of the Rules

When participating in sailboat racing you accept that the decisions according to the Racing Rules, including Appeals etc. described in the *Rules*, are final and cannot be referred to a court of law. See also the definition of Rules.

5   Rules Governing Organizing Authorities and Officials
A race committee may not change, or refuse to implement, the decision of a protest committee, including a decision based on a report from an authority qualified to resolve questions of measurement. See Case 66.

✹*214*

6   World Sailing Regulations
Anti-doping. Be careful what drugs you take. Many non-prescription drugs are banned.

PART 2 – WHEN BOATS MEET

This is the trickiest part of the Racing Rules, and so we will spend some time in examining cases in detail.

Remember that if you are racing and meet another boat racing, these Racing Rules apply. It does not matter if the boats are in different races. If you are not sure that the other boat is racing then the International Regulations for Preventing Collisions at Sea apply (IRPCAS otherwise known as 'Rules of the Road at Sea'), which all normal shipping has to recognise. These regulations always take precedence if there is any doubt. See Case 67. The IRPCAS 10, Traffic Separation Schemes also always apply when racing under the Racing Rules.

✹*215*

Take note that the IRPCAS could be enforced in a race held between sunset and sunrise if so stated in the Notice of Race. See Case 38. See also Case 109 for a further interpretation of the relationship between IRPCAS and the Racing Rules of Sailing.

✹*215*

In order to settle any damage claims, the result of a boat racing protest is normally binding on two boats racing. If one or both boats are not racing then liability depends on the IRPCAS. See also Rule 3.

Note that the penalty limitations in the preamble of Part 2 only apply to the rules of Part 2, except Rule 23.1. Before you go afloat you should study the Sailing Instructions very carefully because you can be disqualified if you fail at any time to keep any of the other rules for a particular race or event. For example, you may be required to carry some special flag in your rigging; you may be required to wear lifejackets; there may be some special instructions going to and from the race area; or you may have to carry extra buoyancy.

> To help you identify the numbers of a particular rule in Part 2, refer to the Fast Find Diagram on page 4

Section A – Right of way

10 On Opposite Tacks

Port and starboard incidents without contact are very common. There is no requirement in the Rules for the onus to be on the port tack boat to prove he was clear of the starboard tack boat but conversely there is nothing in the Rules to suggest that the starboard tack boat should hit the port tack boat to prove her point. See Case 50.

216✷

216/ 225✷

Cases 23, 30, 43 and 88 contain further interpretations of this rule.

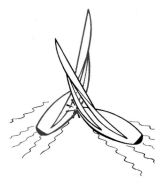

10 On Opposite Tacks

Black has the wind coming from the starboard side and Red has the wind from the port side. Thus Red should keep clear of Black.

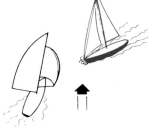

10 & Changing Course
16

Red must not luff to try to hit Black, who would otherwise have been able to keep clear. This case comes under Rule 16.1.

10 &
12 Even though Black is 'overtaking' Red (Fig 1), the definition of 'clear astern' has no relevance because they are on opposite tacks and so Rule 10 and not Rule 12 applies. Red must give way because Black is on starboard tack.

Fig 1

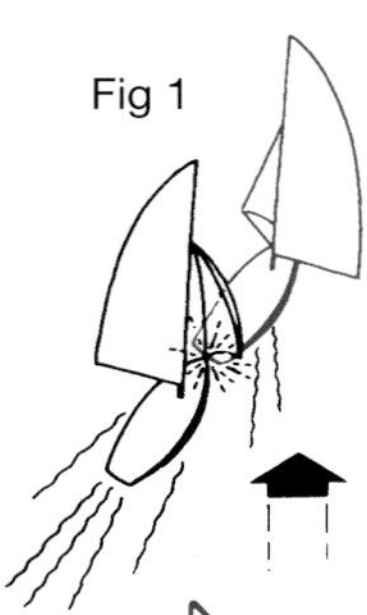

10 &
19 Here (Fig 2) they are at a continuing obstruction. Rule 19.1 says that 19 always applies at a continuing obstruction and 18 does not. However 19.2a is not relevant. Rule 19.2b only applies when they are overlapped and 19.2c only applies if Black was keep clear boat. They are on opposite tacks so Black has right-of-way on starboard under Rule 10. Red should gybe to protect herself. See also Case 30.

*225

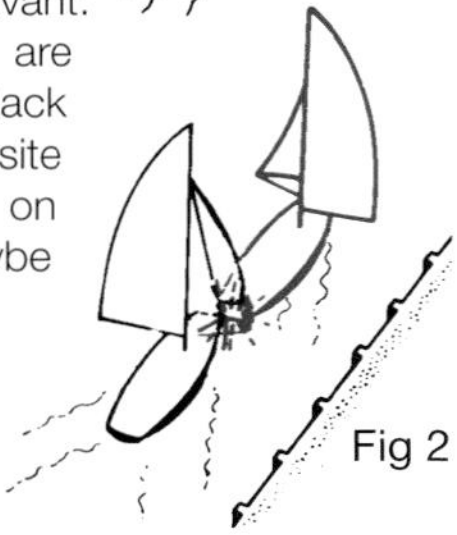

Fig 2

11 **On the Same Tack, Overlapped**
Red is the windward boat (Fig 3) and therefore has to keep clear of Black, including giving her 'wriggle room'. See also explanation to definition of Keep Clear.

Further examples are covered in Cases 7, 13, 14, 24, 25, 51, 70, 73 and 74.

Fig 3

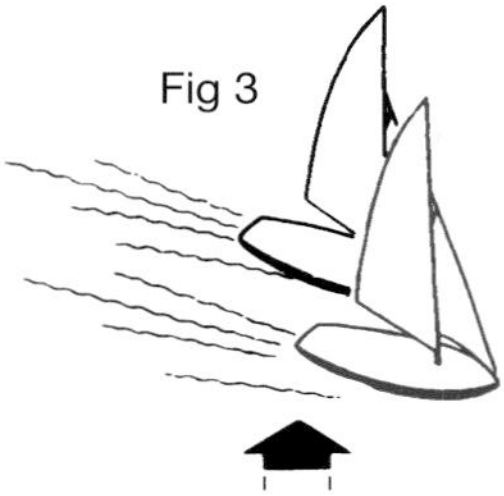

*219
*217
*212
*222
*214

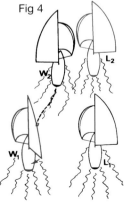

Fig 4

10 & 16   Changing Course
W and L are running parallel, overlapped, on port tack (Fig 4). W gybes on to starboard. Rule 15 applies only briefly after W becomes right-of-way boat. If the boats now sail parallel for some time, L is no longer protected by Rule 15. However W must still be very careful when she changes her course as she must give L room under Rule 16. If W can continue on her course

L is keeping clear. If W changes course she must give room but L must also react immediately to keep clear. See Case 105.

*221

11 & Same Tack, Definition: Keeping Clear and
16   Changing Course

Black can luff slowly head to wind. She has to give Red room to keep clear when she luffs (Rule 16.1), but Red has to keep clear as windward boat (Rule 11) and this includes keeping clear so Black can change course (luff) without immediately making contact (def. Keep Clear). Case 52 is relevant in a match race situation.

220

11   On the Same Tack,
         Overlapped

Black may luff slowly head to wind, even if Red is forced over the line early. Black must give Red enough time and room to keep clear. After the start signal, Black's rights depend on her proper course and how the overlap was established. See Rule 17 and Case 13.

217

11   Overlapped and Definition:
         Keep Clear

Under the definition of Keep Clear, Red can bear away to cover Black but she must keep a distance that not only allows Black to sail her course but also allows Black to luff or bear away without immediately making contact ('wriggle room').

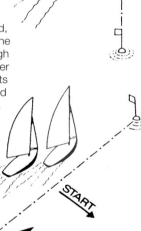

START

156

page

11 & Proper Course and
17 Definitions

Before the starting signal there is no proper course; after the signal Rule 17 applies depending on how the overlap was established. Black can luff slowly head to wind and Red has to keep clear.

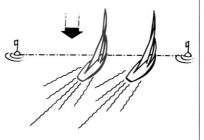

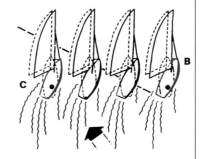

11 & Changing Course
16

Even if C has the right of way under Rule 11 and is not prohibited by Rule 17 to sail above proper course, in practice her possibility to luff is very limited when there are more boats to windward. Under Rule 16.1 she must give the windward boats room to keep clear when she is changing course. If there are several boats to windward it might not be possible for C to luff at all because of the delay in response from the other boats. B and C are still overlapped because of the boats 'between'. See definition Clear astern, Overlap. See Case 114 Question 2.

*221

12 On the Same Tack, Not Overlapped

Red must keep clear and must not sail into Black's stern, if they are on the same tack.

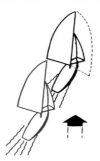

page

217❋

13 While Tacking

This boat has no rights until she reaches a close-hauled course. She is on close-hauled even if the sail is not full because the mainsheet is too loose. Whether the boat has movement through the water or not, is irrelevant. See Case 17.

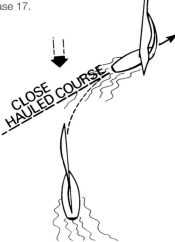

13 While Tacking,
14 Avoiding Contact and
15 Acquiring Right of Way

Red tacks on to starboard and must come on a close-hauled course before she can claim right of way over Black. Black does not have to begin to give way until Red is on a close-hauled course and she is not required to anticipate that Red will break a rule. See Case 27.

218❋

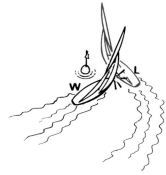

Rules 13, 14, 15 & 16

page

13 Tacking
14 Avoiding Contact
15 Acquiring Right of Way and
16 Changing Course

Here Black bore away to pass under Red's stern. When Red saw this she tacked. There was a collision and Red was wrong under Rule 13 (While Tacking).

Rule 10 ceased to apply when Red passed head to wind and thus stopped being the right-of-way boat.

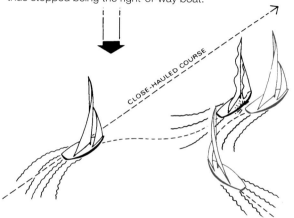

Red became right-of-way boat again when she came on close-hauled, but in such a case Black would not have to **begin** to take avoiding action until Red was on close-hauled (or when it is clear that Red is not keeping clear, Rule 14) and Red shall initially give Black room to keep clear (Rule 15). Had Red been able to tack coming on close-hauled in an ample distance to the leeward of Black, Red would have been in the clear. See Case 6.

✱*219*

13 Two Boats Tacking

In this case the Red boat, which is on Black's port side, must give way. Remember it like this 'If you are on the right – you are in the right!'

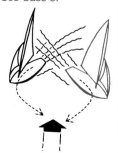

page

Section B – General Limitations

14 Avoiding Contact

Any boat shall avoid contact, and can be penalised for not trying to avoid it, even if she has right of way. If the right-of-way boat tries to avoid contact and fails, and the contact does not result in damage 'that would ordinarily be promptly repaired', then she is still in the clear. However, if the contact causes damage, a right-of-way boat can still be penalised. For interpretation of 'damage' and 'injury' see Cases 19 and 110.

*218/
230*
233*

When a right-of-way boat becomes obliged by Rule 14 to 'avoid contact ... if reasonably possible' and the only way to do so is to 'crash-gybe' and risk damage to herself, she does not break the rule if she does not gybe. See Case 99. Not keeping a lookout may result in failing to avoid contact. See Case 107.

230
218

There is no rule that demands hailing before an unforeseen alteration of course, but hailing could still be one way of 'avoiding contact with another boat if reasonably possible', so it is wise to hail. Cases 14, 23, 26, 30, 50, 54, 87, 92 and 123 contain further interpretations of this rule.

212
216
218
225
226
220

15 Acquiring Right of Way by establishing an Overlap from Clear Astern

Before the start the Red boat came from astern with better speed. Red obtained the overlap too close to Black, who was not given enough room by Red to luff to keep clear. Red is wrong under Rule 15. See Case 53.

219

For a situation with 2 boats coming from clear astern into a line of starting boats see Case 117.

219

15 Acquiring Right of Way by establishing an Overlap

In this case Red has also overtaken Black and has initially given too little room for Black to be able to luff and keep clear, because Black's stern will swing to port as she luffs. See also Cases 7 and 24.

219

page

15 Acquiring Right of Way
11 Overlapped and
17 Same Tack Proper Course

The Black boat is overtaking. From the moment that Black gains an overlap the Red boat becomes the 'windward' boat. She must then start to luff far enough so that Black does not touch her boom, but she need not luff any further because Black must not sail above her proper course. See Cases 7 and 24.

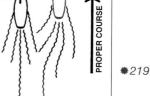

✳*219*

15 Acquiring Right of Way by Gybing

When Red gybes she gains right of way and can force Black to alter course. However here Red has gybed too late and must initially give Black room to keep clear.

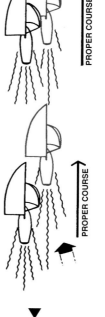

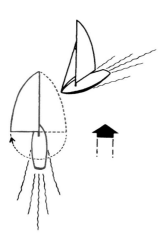

15 **Acquiring Right of Way by Tacking and**

13 **While Tacking**

Red is coming on port tack and is tacking on to starboard tack. Until Red is on close-hauled she shall keep clear under Rule 13. After Red is on close-hauled she must initially give Black room to keep clear under Rule 15. Black does not have to start to luff until after 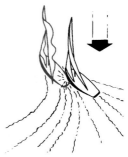 this moment (except to avoid a collision) and is therefore right under Rules 13 and 15 (but maybe breaks Rule 14).

15 **Acquiring Right of Way**

Black completes the tack clear ahead of Red. A hail from Black when she is close-hauled will clarify the moment when she gains the right to force Red to start keeping clear. Red does not have to start any avoiding action until Black is on close-hauled, unless it is clear that there will be contact if she does not act before (Rule 14 Avoiding Contact).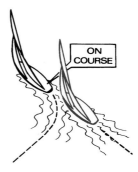

ON COURSE

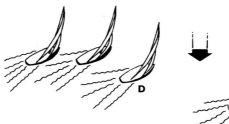

D

15 **Acquiring Right of Way**

In this situation, if the Red boat tacks there is no possibility of D being able to clear Red after Red has completed her tack, and D cannot tack herself because of the proximity of the other boats. If Red tacks, she has not satisfied Rule 15. If the Red boat was to tack on to starboard she would have to bear away astern of D.

15 Acquiring Right of Way
20 Room to Tack at an Obstruction

In this situation if the Black boat (on the right) tacks, the Red boat can only bear away (and give room to B and A under Rule 19.2 if they have an overlap). Red has been given room to keep clear under Rule 15 but there is no time for B and A to respond to a hail from Red before a collision, as required by Rule 20.1(a). So she cannot hail for room to tack.

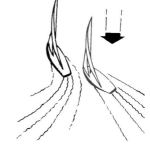

15 Acquiring Right of Way
13 While Tacking and
14 Avoiding Contact

What does the protest committee do? Red protests. Black is the give-way boat before the tack (Rule 10) while tacking (Rule 13) and she has initially to give room to Red (Rule 15). In the rules there is no onus on Black to prove that she was not too close. However the protest committee will often go with Red, first because Black created the situation and second, to stress the importance of the 'basic' rules. So it is easy for Red to put in a protest in a case like this, even if Black was not very close. Black should keep this in mind before making the manoeuvre (or have good witnesses). On the other hand, if Red can touch Black without bearing away, she ought to win the protest. Red does not have to begin to luff clear until Black is on a close-hauled course except to avoid contact.

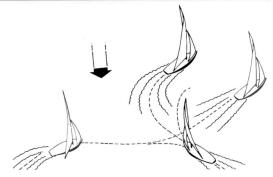

16.1 & Changing Course
16.2

Red has borne away to pass under Black's stern. In order to avoid breaking Rule 16.2, Black must neither luff to tack nor bear away in order to make it difficult for Red to keep clear ('hunting') if this means that Red would immediately need also to change course to keep clear. When the boats get even closer, so that any change of course from Black would deny Red room to keep clear, Black would also break Rule 16.1. If Black does not start to luff for her tack until Red can pass behind her without changing course further, Black would not break Rule 16 but must keep clear while tacking. There may be some doubt as to the actual change of course from Black, but if it is clear that Black has changed her course the onus will be on Black to show that Red did not immediately have to alter course further to keep clear. Red only has to act on the course Black is steering at the time to keep clear. She is not supposed to expect Black to 'hunt' and subsequently change her course. See Case 92.

220✸

16.1 & Changing Course
16.2 and
13 While Tacking

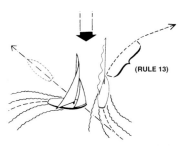

(RULE 13)

If the Red boat luffs head to wind and Black must immediately change course to keep clear, Red can be disqualified under Rule 16.2 and maybe also 16.1, depending on the distances between the boats. If she goes further and tacks, she can be disqualified under both Rules 16 and 13, depending on where the incident actually occurred. See also Case 6.

219✸

16 Changing Course to Start

Red is trying to make a port tack start. Even if Black is right-of-way she must remember that if she luffs at the signal to assume proper course she must give Red room to keep clear under Rule 16. If Red has timed her start perfectly and is on a steady course that would keep her clear of Black before Black luffs, she is OK, but it is a risky manoeuvre for Red. *Note!* there is no rule that allows Black to assume proper course even if this prevents Red from keeping clear.

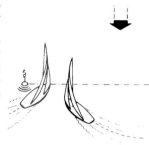

16, 18.1 & 18.2(c) and Definition: Mark-Room

Red takes the mark rather wide and tacks. Black is clear astern but rounds tighter and can touch Red. When Red tacked, Rule 18.2(b) no longer applied (Rule 18.2(c) so Red is no longer entitled to mark-room. The boats are now on opposite tacks so Rule 18 does not apply (Rule 18.1). Red must give way under Rules 13 and 10, but if Red could have kept clear of Black while tacking and after getting on port tack, had Black not changed her course round the mark, Red is protected by Rule 16. **Note!** When Rule 18 does not apply there is no rule that allows Black to assume proper course rounding a mark and the tack is not part of the mark-room she is entitled to under the definition.

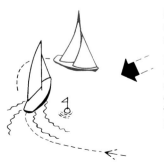

See Case 76 for a situation where the starboard boat is changing course at a windward finishing mark.

✹221

If a right-of-way boat alters course in such a way that the give-way boat, in spite of prompt avoiding action, still cannot keep clear by her own efforts then the right-of-way boat breaks Rule 16. See Case 60.

✹220

page

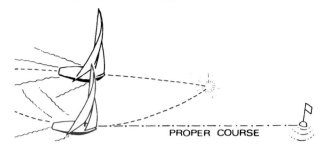

PROPER COURSE

17   On the Same Tack; Proper Course

Red establishes her overlap by diving through the Black boat's lee but must not sail above her proper course whilst the overlap lasts. If there is a dispute about what is Red's proper course then the Black boat must keep clear and protest. See Cases 14 and 46, and also explanations of Proper Course.

212❋

17   On the Same Tack; Proper Course
Definition: Clear Astern

Black is overtaking Red and is the give-way boat because she is on port. As soon as her bow crosses Red's 'transom-line', she may gybe and then gains the right to sail above proper course. If Black was overtaking on the same tack as Red, then she could gain the right by doing two quick gybes.

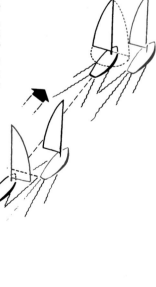

PROPER COURSE

17 On the Same Tack; Sail
& 18.4 above Proper Course

The boats are in the zone so Rule 18 applies but both rules give the same result. Black must gybe (under Rule 17 if the overlap was established from clear astern and always under Rule 18.4), because gybing is the only way she can avoid sailing above or further from the mark than her proper course. See also Case 75.

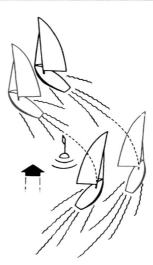

✹225

17 On the Same Tack;
Proper Course and
Two Hull Lengths

Black is inside a distance of two of her hull lengths from Red. It is two hull lengths of the leeward boat and the two-length limitation applies only to this rule. The measurement of the two hull lengths' distance is taken from hull to hull as shown.

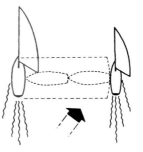

17
& 11

Same Tack Overlapped

Black is overtaking Red with better speed on a steady course, which is slightly higher than the course to the next mark. She is not 'changing course'. Red should call 'Overlap!' and thus Black cannot sail above proper course, as this overlap exists. Black is *not* obliged to bear away to the mark. She is actually sailing *her* 'proper course', and Rule 11 applies. If Red thinks that Black is sailing above her proper course, her only remedy is to keep clear and protest. See also definition of Proper Course and Case 14.

212 ❋

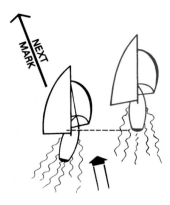

17,
11 &
12

Stopping a Luff

It is clever to call 'No overlap!' or something similar, as soon as the overlap is broken, because this is the best way to stop the leeward boat sailing above her proper course. When Red becomes clear ahead the Black boat must keep clear under Rule 12 and Red can bear away to her proper course. When the overlap is re-established it will be from clear astern so even if Black is again right-of-way she cannot sail above her proper course. Black can only regain her right to sail above her proper course if she creates a new overlap by drawing clear ahead or more than two lengths abeam, or by doing two quick gybes.

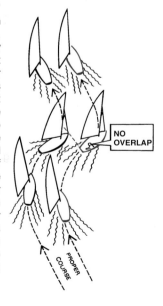

Section C – At Marks and Obstructions

All Rules in this section cover special cases. When these cases apply they sometimes limit the actions of the right-of-way boat under the basic rules that precede them in Section A of Part 2. See Preamble of Part 2 Section A. **Note** that according to the Preamble of Section C these rules do **not** apply at a starting mark surrounded by navigable water from the time that boats are approaching the marks to start until they have passed them.

18   Mark-Room

This is one of the most important rules, as it is the one that is involved most frequently. It is set out in two parts.

18.1   Instructions on where the rule applies, and special situations where it does not (or where only part of it applies).

Remember that according to the Preamble, Rule 18 as a rule in Section C does not apply at a starting mark when approaching to start. Also it does not apply in the four situations mentioned in Rule 18.1:

a) on opposite tacks on a beat to windward (see 'on a beat to windward' Case 132);

❋*230*

b) between boats on opposite tacks when the proper course for one but not both of them is to tack;

c) between a boat approaching a mark and one leaving it and

d) if the mark is a continuing obstruction, in which case Rule 19 applies.

**18.2
18.3 &
18.4**   The rule itself with instructions for giving mark-room and keeping clear when rounding, including what happens if one boat tacks or has to gybe.

18.1 Preamble

Rule 18 applies when at least one boat is in the zone of a mark with a required side. This means that the rule starts to apply and the overlap relations are determined at the same time. The old discussions on when a boat was 'about to round' and when Rule 18 started to apply are gone.

Taking an 'Inside' Boat the Wrong Side of a Mark

If you wish to take a windward boat to the wrong side of the mark you may do so, but (1) both boats must remain outside the zone of the mark and (2) you must have the right to sail above proper course (Rule 17).

Section C Preamble Not Rule 18 at a Starting Mark

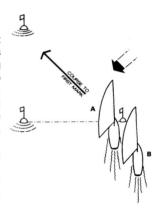

B has no right to mark-room at a starting mark. Rule 11 covers the situation. Until the starting signal, A can sail up to head to wind and B must keep clear. As soon as the starting gun has fired, A must not sail above proper course if her overlap was established from clear astern (Rule 17) and must not squeeze B out by sailing higher than this. If there is still not enough room for B then A is not obliged to sail lower than proper course because Rule 18 does *not* apply at a starting mark, but 17 does. If, however, A sails a course that leaves space for B to sail between A and the mark and B sails into the room freely given and A then luffs and B to keep clear is compelled to touch the mark A's luff breaks Rule 16.1. See Case 114 Question 3.

221 ✳

Section C Preamble; Not Rule 18 at a starting mark

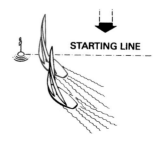

STARTING LINE

Black cannot claim mark-room at a starting mark under Rule 18. However Black has the right under Rule 11 to luff and try to 'shoot the mark', as long as she gives Red room to keep clear as provided by Rule 16.1 and does not pass head to wind.

Section C Preamble

11 & 17 Yacht C can neither claim mark-room between boat D and the mark under Rule 18 before the starting gun nor afterwards. Rules 11 and, after the starting gun, 17 applies. A is head to wind and has the right to do this before and after the starting gun if the overlap was *not* established from clear astern. After the signal he must not sail above proper course if she established the overlap from clear astern. Rule 11 and 17 cover the situation.

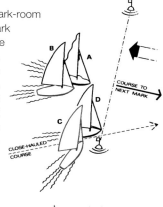

18.1(a) Not on Opposite Tacks on a Beat to Windward

This clause says that Rule 18 does not apply in this situation because the two

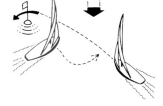

boats are sailing on a beat to windward on opposite tacks. Rule 10 applies, and so Black does not have to give mark-room to Red to round a mark inside her. For when boats are 'on a beat to windward' See Case 132.

✳*230*

18.1(a) Opposite Tacks
18.3 Tacking When Approaching a Mark

Red cannot claim mark-room under rule 18.2 while luffing up to head to wind (Rule 18.1(a)) nor after turning past head to wind (Rule 13) though she has right of way before (Rule 10). After the tack she is subject to Rule 18.3 since Black is 'fetching' the mark. If Red chooses to sail past the mark Black must keep clear under Rule 10. It is exactly the same as if they were in the middle of the course with no mark anywhere near. Remember it like this: at the windward mark on opposite tacks 'Take the mark away'. See also Case 9.

✳*222*

page

18.2(a) Overlapped

222✳

Red shall give mark-room to Black, assuming Black made her overlap in time. Red must give mark-room even though the boats are on widely differing courses. See Case 12.

18.2(a) Overlapped and Definition: Mark-Room

222✳

Black must have enough mark-room to be able to gybe without being obstructed by Red, because to gybe is part of sailing her proper course to round the mark. Red must still give mark-room even if Black's gybe breaks the overlap. See also Case 21 for interpretations of 'room' and 'mark-room'.

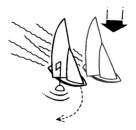

18.2(a) Overlapped and Definitions: Mark-Room and Room

Black must have mark-room including room to tack, since her proper course is to sail close to the mark (definition Mark-Room (a)), a tack is 'necessary to sail the course' (definition Mark-Room (b)) and Black is overlapped inside and after a tack she can fetch the next mark (definition Mark-Room last sentence). If Black's genoa touched Red when it was freed off for the tack, for example, Red would not have given enough mark-room. Under the definition 'Room' Black is entitled to space to tack 'promptly in a seamanlike way'. If the mark is rounded as start of a 'windward leg', Black is not entitled to room to tack since the tack is not 'necessary to sail the course' (definition Mark-Room (b)). From the moment Black has rounded the mark and is on a close-hauled course she is no longer entitled to mark-room. Rule 11 applies and Black is the windward boat. She must keep clear and can not claim room for a tack that she wants to make for tactical reasons. See Case 25.

NEXT MARK

217✳

page

18.2 Giving Mark-Room
(a+b+c) Black enters the zone before Red and, when Black enters, she is clear astern of Red. Therefore, Rule 18.2(b) does not

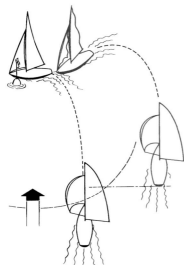

apply because neither of its conditions was met when the first boat (Black) entered the zone. When Red turns towards the mark, an overlap begins with Black inside. At that moment, Rule 18.2(a) applies and requires Red to give Black mark-room. After Red becomes clear astern of Black, Rule 18.2(a) no longer applies. However Rule 12 does and it requires Red to keep clear of Black. If Red becomes overlapped inside she must give Black Room to sail her proper course (Rule 18.2 (c) (2)).

See also Cases 2 and 59.

✻*223*

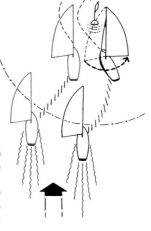

CURRENT

18.2 Giving Mark-Room,
(a+b+c) Overlapped
Black has an overlap in time so Rules 18.2(b) and 18.2(c) apply. Even if Black gybes, or for some reason loses the overlap, Rule 18.2(c) says that Black can still claim mark-room to round inside.

18.2(a) Overlapped

Red is not within the zone of the mark when she alters course and thus 'gives' Black an overlap when Red enters the zone. She cannot refuse to give Black mark-room, because the overlap is established in time. However see also 18.2(d) if there is doubt about establishing an overlap in time.

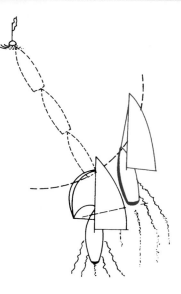

18.2(a), 11, 17.1 and Definition: Mark-Room

If Black has established her overlap outside the zone, or because of Red tacking on top, Red must keep clear (Rule 11) and give mark-room (Rule 18.2(a) or (b)). Even if Rule 17 also applies between them, Black can luff above close-hauled to 'shoot the mark'. This is her 'proper course' so Red has to give mark-room under Rule 18 and is give-way boat both according to Rules 11 and 17.

If this mark was to be rounded to starboard, at the moment shown in the diagram, Black is breaking Rule 18.2 because she is not giving Red mark-room which includes room to sail *to* the mark. See Cases 70 and 118.

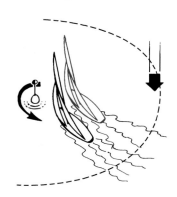

222

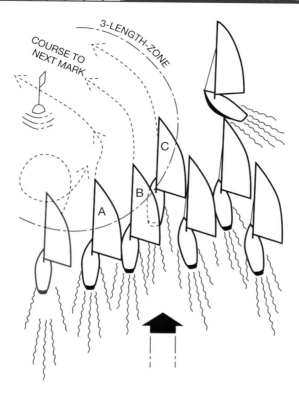

18.2(a+e) Giving Mark-Room

When C enters the zone she must give B room including
the space B needs to give room to A etc. See Case 114
Question 1. However even though Red has established an
overlap before C entered the zone, A may not be able to
give mark-room because of the delay in response from the
outside boats. If the next boat is not able to give mark-room
at the time when the overlap begins, she is not required to
give it according to Rule 18.2(e).

18.2(b) Clear ahead at the Zone
43.1(b) Exoneration

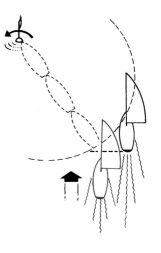

Black is allowed to make a normal smooth rounding. She is within the zone of the mark and clear ahead of Red and so she does not have to give mark-room inside and is entitled to mark-room. Also Rule 43.1(b) gives her protection when she is sailing to the mark and, provided she is sailing her proper course, when she is altering course to round at the mark.

Black is protected under Rules 18.2(b+c) and 43.1(b) until she no longer needs mark-room.

If Black makes a bad rounding, maybe because of boats ahead of her, and gives Red room, Red may try to round inside, but at her own risk. Black may try to 'close the door' on Red by luffing, but Black's mark-room does not include room to sail above her proper course so a luff above proper course may not be so rapid that it breaks Rule 16.1. See Case 63.

224❋

18.2(b) Giving Mark-Room
43.1(b) Exoneration

Black entered the zone clear ahead and turned abruptly to round. Red must keep clear even though she now has an

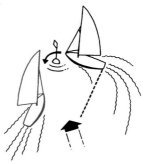

overlap since this was not made in time. Neither can Red claim her starboard tack rights because Black is inside the zone and Rule 18 limits the actions of Red as right-of-way boat under Rule 10 and she must give mark-room under 18.2(b+c). Even if Black breaks a rule of Section A or Rule 15 or 16 rounding on her proper course, she shall be exonerated under Rule 43.1(b).

18.2(b) Not Overlapped

Black, who is clear ahead, has the right to gybe. This is part of her mark-room sailing her proper course to round the mark; so Red must give mark-room until Black has gybed and passed the mark.

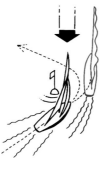

18.2   Clear at the zone,
(b+c) and Definition Mark-Room
13   While Tacking

Red is clear ahead but cannot claim room to tack because 18.2 last sentence says that if she passes head to wind Rule 18.2(b) no longer applies and the definition of mark-room last sentence does not give her room to tack. So Rule 13 applies if she passes head to wind. See Case 15. The rights are the same if the situation is reversed to a starboard rounding. See Case 81.

*224

18.2(b+c+d)
18.1   While Tacking and
16   Changing Course

If Black is far enough ahead to be able to turn from head to wind to a close-hauled starboard course without Red having to change course and, thereafter, Red has room to keep clear, Black may do so. Black has right-of-way while she luffs. When she passes head to wind, Rule 18.2(b) ceases to apply according to 18.2(c). They are now on opposite tacks and one (Red) has to change tack to round so Rule 18 does not apply according to Rule 18.1. Black becomes give-way under Rule 13, but Red must, from this moment under Rule 16, not change her course to prevent Black from keeping clear. See Case 15.

*224

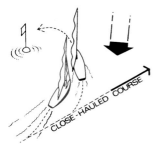

CLOSE-HAULED COURSE

18.2 Clear ahead at the Zone

(b+c) The course is from a reach to a reach. W clear ahead luffs head to wind. L must give W mark-room under Rule 18.2(b). After L has steered to pass under W's stern then W can tack and continue.

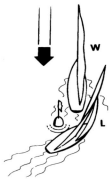

18.2(d) Giving Mark-Room

We all know how boats surge back and forth relative to each other on waves. If there is doubt about an overlap being broken or established just at the moment when the leading boat is entering the zone, it shall be presumed that the situation is not changed, ie you go back to a situation where there was no doubt. So you could say that the doubt (and the protest committee) will go against the boat that claims to have changed the situation, and gained an advantage in the very last moment (unless she has very good witnesses). Red is surfing on a wave with good speed; Red should not risk trying to establish an inside overlap even if Black was still just outside the zone, because the doubt will go against Red.

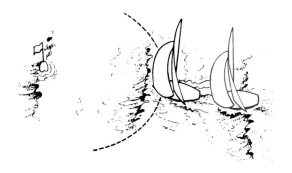

18.3 Tacking when Approaching a Mark and Definition: Fetching

Red changed tack within the zone. Black is 'fetching' the mark because she can round the mark without any more tacks. Rule 18.3 says that Rule 18.2 does not apply so Red is not entitled to mark-room, furthermore Red will break Rule 18.3(a) if she causes Black to sail above close-hauled.

This also applies if the boats were both originally on port tack and Black tacked outside the zone without breaking Rule 13 or 15. See Case 95.

✴*224*

When two boats tack to starboard inside. See Case 133.

✴*224*

If the mark were to be rounded to starboard 18.3 would not apply. Also Black would not be fetching the mark even if she is on the layline because she would need one more tack to round the mark. Rules 11, 13, 15 and 18.2(a) would govern the situation. Black would be entitled to mark-room after Red completed the tack.

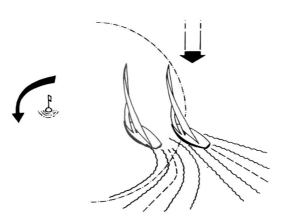

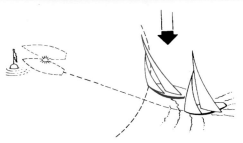

18.3(b) Tacking when Approaching a Mark

Red changed tack and became subject to Rule 13 in the zone. Black had right of way before the tack (Rule 10) and during the tack (Rule 13). After the tack Rule 18.2 does not apply but Black is entitled to mark-room because of Rule 18.3(b). Black becomes overlapped to leeward of Red so Red shall also keep clear under Rule 11. If Black is clear astern when Red completes the tack and then establishes an overlap by sailing her course, Rule 15 does not apply since it was Red's 'action' that gave Black right of way. If Black bore away to establish a leeward overlap, Rule 15 does apply since Black acquired right of way by her own 'action'.

If however Red completes the tack and gives mark-room when Black establishes an overlap and Black then luffs, Rule 16 applies to Black. See Case 93.

Had Red tacked outside the zone and Black then had an overlap when the first boat entered the zone the situation had been the same except that Black would also be entitled to mark-room under Rule 18.2.

224❋

18.3(b) Tacking when Approaching a Mark

Red tacks within the zone. Black becomes overlapped inside. Black give mark-room under Rule 18.3(b), so Red cannot deny she was the first to reach the zone and passed ahead of Black.

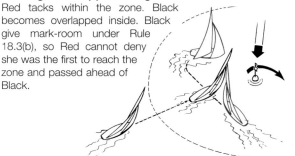

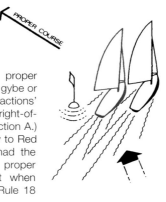

18.4 Gybing

Red must gybe on to her proper course. Black can choose to gybe or continue. This rule 'limits the actions' of Red even if she is the right-of-way boat. (See Preamble Section A.) Even if Rule 17 did not apply to Red and, therefore, she earlier had the right to sail (luff) above her proper course, she lost that right when they entered the zone and Rule 18 started to apply.

18.4 Gybing and Preamble Part 2 Section A

Red must gybe and sail no further from the mark than is needed to sail her proper course to round the mark. She is not allowed to continue and force the others to keep clear even if she is on starboard tack. Rule 18.4 applies (see also the definition Clear Astern etc) and limits the actions of Red under Rule 10. See Case 75.

*225

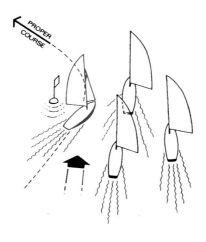

page

19.1   When Rule 19 Applies

When does Rule 19 start to apply? Rule 19.1 says 'at' the obstruction and that means Rule 19.1 applies when either of the overlapped boats is alongside the obstruction. Also, note that the definition 'zone' does not apply at obstructions – only at marks, and Rule 19 does not (like Rule 18 and Definition Mark-Room) allow room to sail 'to' the obstruction. If the boats are not overlapped, Rule 19 does *not* apply unless it is a continuing obstruction and a boat clear astern which is required to keep clear becomes overlapped inside. Then Rule 19.2(c) applies.

19.2
(a+b)   Giving Room at an Obstruction
20   Room to Tack at an Obstruction

The starboard tack boat is an obstruction. Red can choose to tack or to bear away under Rule 19.2(a) because she has right of way over B as the leeward boat under Rule 11. If she chooses to tack then Rule 20 applies. If she chooses to bear away, Rule 19 applies, and she has to give room to boat B who is overlapping 'inside'. There is no 'zone' around S so Red only has to give room when she is 'at' the obstruction, so in this situation if a late bear-away from Red breaks the overlap, B is not entitled to room. See also Rule 20 and Cases 3 and 11.

226/
225❋

225❋

For a situation with three boats on port see Case 125.

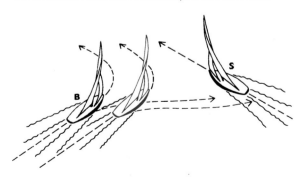

19.2 Giving Room at an Obstruction
(a+b) The boat not racing is crossing the course, and Red has the choice of which side to pass as leeward right-of-way boat. She must however give Black (overlapping inside) room to pass on the same side as herself when she chooses to go below.

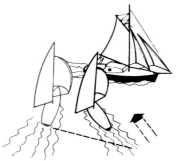

19.2 Approaching an obstruction.
It is the right-of-way boat at any time who can choose which side to pass. See Case 124.

※225

19.2(b) Unable to Give Room at an Obstruction when the overlap began and Definition: Obstruction.
L is an obstruction to M but not a continuing obstruction according to the definition even if the boats are moving at almost the same speed. M is going slightly faster but can only establish an overlap from clear astern if W is able to give room when the overlap begins. If W is not able to give room for M to pass between her and L because of other boats close to windward of her, she need not give M room. If W is not restricted she must give room between her and L for M to pass but Rules 15 and 17 apply to M when she establishes the overlap.

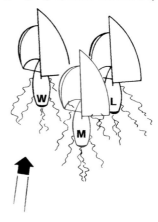

page

19.2(c) Giving Room at a Continuing Obstruction

This is an awkward rule to interpret. Presumably the leading boat is already as close to the obstruction as she thinks she can go with safety. Therefore it is difficult for the overtaking boat to show that she can safely go closer.

However, even if Black is 'at' the obstruction, Red can try for an overlap under this rule, but it is risky and if protested, Red will have to establish that there was room to pass inside. If however an overlap is established correctly, Black cannot luff Red ashore but must, if necessary, even bear off to give Red room.

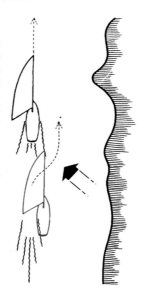

225 ❋

See also Cases 29 and 33 for further interpretations of this rule.

19.2(c) Giving Room at a Continuing Obstruction

Black must be careful when arriving at a break in the obstruction. This is Red's chance to establish an overlap.

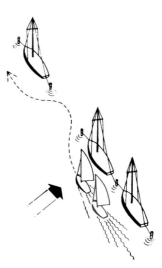

20 Room to Tack at an Obstruction

When does the rule apply? Note that the definition 'zone' does not apply to obstructions only marks. Rule 20 permits a boat to hail for 'room to tack and avoid another boat on the same tack' (Preamble 20.1) when the hailing boat is not 'sailing below close-hauled' (Rule 20.1(b)) and if she cannot 'avoid the obstruction safely without making a substantial course change' (Rule 20.1(a)). When these criteria are fulfilled the rule applies. If the obstruction is a mark that the hailed boat can fetch see Rule 20.1(c). However if a boat hails, the hailed boat *must* respond no matter what. If she thinks the hail is invalid she must still respond according to Rule 20.2 and her only remedy is to protest that the conditions in Rule 20.1 Hailing was not fulfilled. Maybe she is not aware of an obstruction that could be something floating in front of the hailing boat. So you could say the rule always applies but using it to gain a tactical advantage not only breaks Rule 20.1 but could break Rule 2 Fair Sailing and the Basic Principle of Sportsmanship.

20 Room to Tack at an Obstruction

Black can no longer continue in safety, so she hails. Red must tack as soon as possible after she hears Black's hail. Black must give Red time to respond to the hail and then tack as soon as possible after Red. If Black observes no response to her hail, a second hail might be required. See Case 54.

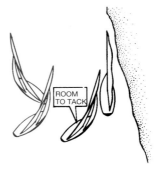

ROOM TO TACK

✻*226*

20 Room to Tack at an Obstruction

Black has the right to call 'Room to tack', but Red can reply 'You tack!', and then she is obliged to keep clear of Black. Black must start to tack as soon as possible after Red's reply hail. Red must remember that in the case of a protest she will have to prove that she has kept clear of Black during her tack.

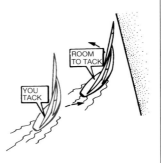

ROOM TO TACK

YOU TACK

20.1
& 20.2 Hailing and Responding

In this case Red is probably able to tack and avoid Black. She has the right to call for room when she is not sure she can clear Black either by passing ahead or by bearing away under her stern. So if it is marginal, Red can call for room to tack. If Black replies 'you tack', then Red *must* tack and Black must give her room while she tacks. When completing her tack to port Red must then keep clear under Rule 10 so if she can clear Black by going astern she must do so and Black has met her obligation under Rule 20.1(b). See Case 35. If, after the tack is completed, Black can force Red to tack back to starboard in a seamanlike way, Red must do so and Black has given the room required. See case 101. For a similar situation but with breakwaters projecting from the shore see Case 33.

226 ✳

225 ✳

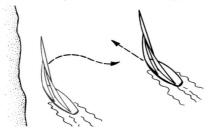

20 Room to Tack at an Obstruction

A can hail C for room to tack because D is an obstruction to A. Boat C must tack (or give A room to tack some other way if possible). It is of no significance whether C can fetch the mark or not, because the mark is not the obstruction. Even if it was a port hand rounding, C cannot claim room at the mark from A under Rule 18. D has starboard right of way over both A and C and is an obstruction to A so Rule 20 and not Rule 18 applies (Rule 20.2(e)). The situation is exactly as if the mark was not there. See Case 3.

226 ✳

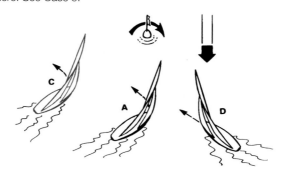

20   Room to Tack at an Obstruction
20.3 Passing on a Hail to an Additional Boat

A can hail B for room to tack because the boat running is an obstruction that requires A to make a substantial course change. B can pass on a hail to tack to C under Rule 20.3 even if Red C herself could have passed the boat running without a substantial course change.

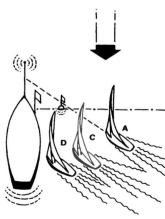

20   and Preamble Section C

Situation 1 The starting line is between two buoys. The starting vessel is not a starting mark but ranks as an obstruction.

In this situation, boat D can hail boat C for room to tack at the obstruction. C can only hail boat A for room to tack because of the starting vessel and not to pass the right side of the starting mark. If boat D were not there, boat C might have been forced to sail over the line between the mark and the starting boat before she could claim room.

Situation 2 The starting vessel is a starting mark, as is the inner limit mark.

Neither boat D nor boat C can claim room to tack from boat A when the obstruction is a starting mark since Rule 20 as part of Section C does not apply at the starting mark or its anchor line according to the preamble of Section C.

20 and Preamble of Section C

The starting vessel forms one end of the line and is therefore a starting mark. The vessel and the anchor line are also obstructions, but according to the Preamble, Red is not entitled to room to tack. The middle boat cannot claim room to tack for the anchor line according to the Preamble. Even though the anchor line is not part of the mark according to the definition of Mark, Rule 18 does not apply at a starting mark or its anchor line so she is not entitled to mark-room to pass under Rule 18 even if she could do so without tacking.

Red only has rights under Rule 11; if the obstruction was not there so she can luff and try to 'shoot' the mark as long as she does not pass head to wind.

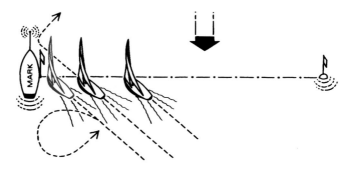

20 and Preamble Section C

In this case the starting line transit is completely on the shore. Both before and after the start signal, Black can hail Red for room to tack because not only is the starting mark not surrounded by navigable water, but also the whole shoreline is an obstruction when they are approaching to start.

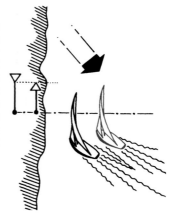

20.1(c) When not to Hail
19.1 When Rule 19 Applies

If Red hails Black for room to tack, Black must give her that room. However, because Black is fetching the mark, such a hail by Red breaks Rule 20.3 so Black can protest

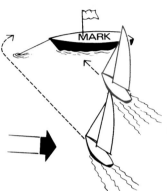

and Red must take a penalty or be disqualified. Because the obstruction is also a mark, Rule 18 applies and Rule 19 does not (see Rule 19.1). Therefore, Black must give Red mark-room if she can 'shoot' the mark without passing head to wind. If Red had been slightly more to windward she would have been able to hail for room to tack under Rule 20 because of the mooring rope that is an obstruction but not part of the mark (see Definition Mark).

20.1(c) Red cannot decline a hail from Black even if she thinks Black is not entitled to hail because Red can fetch the mark. Her only remedy is to respond to the hail and protest. If Black does not hail because Red is obviously fetching, and the wind shifts, Black can still hail as long as Red has time to respond under Rule 20.2.

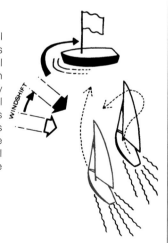

Section D – Other Rules

21.1 Starting Errors

Even though a boat which has started too early is on starboard tack, she has to keep clear of all others – even port tack boats when she sails towards the pre-start side of the line.

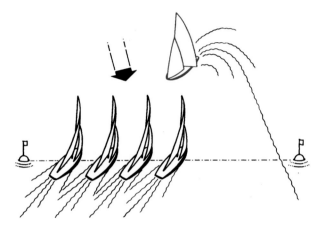

21.1 Starting Errors

Red has started too early and luffs into the wind in order to slow down so that she can drop back and start again. However, she keeps her rights until she is sailing a course towards the pre-start side of the starting line. So A has to keep clear as long as Red is still pointing up wind and not moving astern (Rule 22.3). Red could be luffing to protect herself and not because she was early in the start.

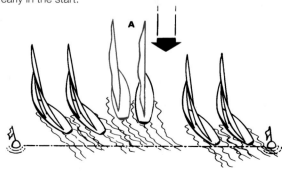

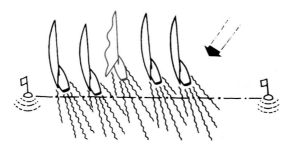

21.1 Starting Errors

The Red boat has started too early but the only thing she can do is let the jib and the mainsail go. She can slow down by backing the sails if she is able without affecting the leeward boat (which has right of way), and without moving astern. As soon as it is clear that she is not making her way up the course and she has begun to decrease the distance to the startline she has begun her manoeuvre of 'sailing towards the pre-start side of the starting line', and she must keep clear of other boats.

21.1 Starting Errors

As soon as the starting signal is made, the Red boats, who are on the wrong side of the line, must keep clear. After the starting signal they have no right of way because they have to comply with Rule 29.1 (individual recall). If Rule 30.1 (I-flag round the ends) applies, they already lose right of way during the last minute before the signal.

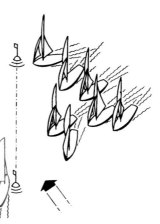

21.1 Starting Errors and
15 Acquiring Right of Way

Even though she has regained her starboard tack rights when she is completely on the pre-start side of the line, the Red boat must now initially give boat A room to keep clear under Rule 15. It will be impossible for boat A to comply in this situation.

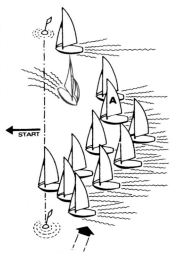

21.3 Backing a sail

A and B are on starboard tack, but they are early in the start. They start moving astern or sideways to windward by deliberately backing a sail. As long as they are moving ahead or still in the water A has right of way over C – starboard (Rule 10), B has right over D – leeward (Rule 11) and E – clear ahead (Rule 12), but as soon as they start moving astern or sideways to windward through the water while backing a sail they become give-way boats. When Rule 21 applies, the rules of Section A do not, according to the preamble of Section D. A boat that goes head to wind with flapping sails and stops, maybe even drifting somewhat astern, does not lose her rights. Only moving astern by backing a sail comes under Rule 21. In match racing Rule 21.3 is deleted (Rule C2.11).

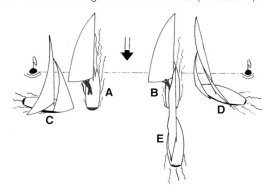

22   Capsized

You have to keep clear of a capsized dinghy until she has regained control. Under the Rules it is the same as if it was an obstruction.

22.1 Starting Errors

Yacht B has started too early and, because of the starboard tack boat, she has to hail boat C for room to tack. Yacht B has the right to do this because she is not yet sailing towards the pre-start side of the starting line. After tacking she can then begin to slow down.

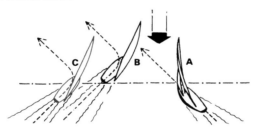

22.2 Taking Penalties

If you are exonerating yourself after touching a mark, or are taking a two-turns penalty, you are on a proper course all the time. However you must keep clear of non-penalised boats when you are making the penalty, ie from when you start the turn until you have done one or two tacks and gybes in the same direction.

23.2 Interfering with another Boat

Case 126 addresses how to determine if boats are on the same leg.

✳*226*

Hailing situations summarised

1 Obligatory hailing situations

(a) Hail for room to tack at an obstruction (Rule 20).). If a hail may not be heard under the conditions a clear signal shall be made. NoR may specify alternative communication.

(b) A protesting boat shall try to inform another boat that she intends to protest. Hailing is mandatory if it is an incident in the racing area and you are within hailing distance (Rule 61.1(a)).

2 Recommended hailing situations

(a) Any situation or manoeuvre where a hail would clarify or support one's case, eg in the establishment or termination of an overlap at a mark or obstruction (Rules 18 and 19) or in a luffing situation (Rule 17).

(b) If a boat needs to be avoided because she is out of control, aground or helping someone in the water (Rule 22) a hail could be relevant to warn other boats.

(c) To avoid a collision, a right-of-way boat may hail before she makes an alteration of course that may not be foreseen by another boat (Rule 16).

(d) A right-of-way boat may hail a boat that seems not to be keeping clear to avoid contact (Rule 14).

PART 3 – CONDUCT OF A RACE

25 Race Signals

In a recall situation, where no sound signal is given, there can be no recall. Race signals must be accompanied by a sound signal when indicated in 'Race Signals'. See Cases 31 and 71.

✳227/
228

25 Race Signals

Always be prepared so that you can recognise signals, in case the Committee stops the race at one of the marks, shortens the course in a special way, or changes a mark as provided in the Sailing Instructions. See the back cover of this book for quick reference. Remember a 'flag' can also be an object with an appearance similar to a flag, like a board or a shape.

26.1 Starting Systems

Note the timing of the start shall be governed by the *visual starting signal*. The timing is made from the flag/shape and not from the gun, bell, whistle or hooter. Even if the sound signal is not made at all, the failure shall be disregarded.

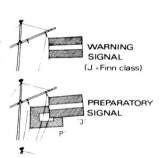

WARNING
SIGNAL
(J = Finn class)

PREPARATORY
SIGNAL

28.1 Sailing the Course and
30.1 I Flag Rule

During a normal start, a boat which is over the line early can re-start like boat D. However, if the 'round-the-ends' Rule 30.1 is invoked (Code flag I was flown), as frequently happens after a general recall, then a boat which is over the line will have to return like boat A.

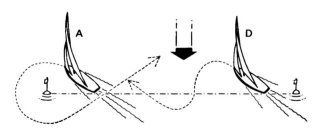

page

211/
227✽

227/
230/
228✽

28.1 Sailing the Course and Definitions

If the sailing instructions say that you should finish by leaving the committee boat to port and, for example, they put the committee boat on the wrong side of the mark, you should follow the finishing definition of the Rules exactly (from the course side), even if you thereby leave the committee boat to starboard and thus violate the sailing instructions. See Cases 45, 82 and 129.

When the 'string' of the track lies on the required side, it does not matter if a mark, a gate or the finish line has been 'looped'. See Cases 106, 108 and 145.

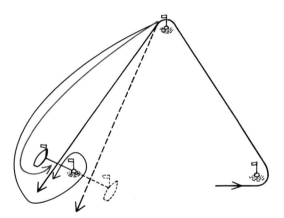

28.1 Sailing the Course

Red has rounded incorrectly. Black is right. You have to unwind yourself before rounding properly.

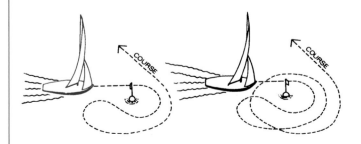

page

28.2 Required Side of Mark

The course is: Start, mark 1, mark 2, mark 3 etc. Both marks 1 and 2 are marks of the course for boat A.

B has just rounded mark 2 and therefore mark 1 is no longer considered as a mark for her.

C has not yet rounded mark 1 and therefore she can please herself which side of mark 2 she goes. She can touch it without infringing. See also Rule 31 and Case 58.

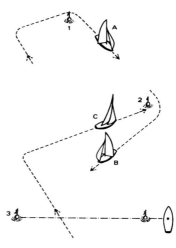

✱227

28.1& Sailing the Course
28.2

A starting mark has a 'required side' when a boat approaches to start, but it must not be touched before the start (Rule 31).

Black must be correct because she has passed the limit mark on the required side when approaching the line to start.

Red is wrong because the mark had already been passed before she was 'approaching the starting line from its pre-start side to start'. For a further interpretation of the 'string' rule see Case 90.

✱227

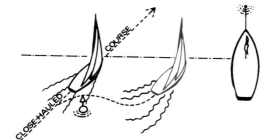

28 Sailing the Course and Definitions: Finishing and Racing

Red, who has crossed the finishing line, still has to keep clear of the starboard tack boats as she is still racing. She can go under their sterns and still maintain her finishing position because she has already finished. She may clear the line in any direction.

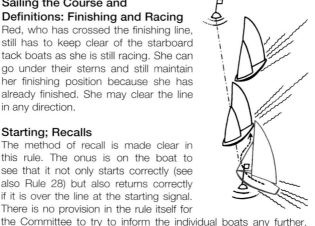

29 Starting; Recalls

The method of recall is made clear in this rule. The onus is on the boat to see that it not only starts correctly (see also Rule 28) but also returns correctly if it is over the line at the starting signal. There is no provision in the rule itself for the Committee to try to inform the individual boats any further. This might even be unfair, as the boats that are informed first can return to start earlier than the boats that are informed later. However Appendix L Sailing Instructions Guide provides for broadcasting sail numbers on VHF if boats are on the course side during the two minutes before the start signal to help avoid a general recall if several boats are early. Cases 31, 71 and 79 contain further interpretations of this rule.

227/
228✹

30.3 Black Flag Rule

Even if a boat believes that the Race Committee has made an error in disqualifying her under this rule and intends to claim redress, she is not entitled to sail in the next race. This is a bit sad because if she is right and is granted redress, it is more difficult for the Race Committee to give a fair redress when the boat has not sailed the race.
See Case 96.

228✹

31 Touching a Mark and Definition: Mark

You can touch the buoy rope with the keel without infringing Rule 31.1. If you foul the rope and it is caught round the keel or rudder you can use your own gear to clear it.

31 Touching a Mark and Definition: Mark

Whether the dinghy is 'intentionally attached' to the Start mark is difficult to know so you should not touch it. But the Race Committee should avoid any confusion and not place a dinghy like this.

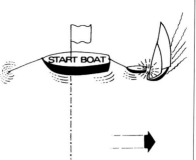

31 Touching a Mark

Once you know you have hit a mark you must do one of three things. Either:

(a) exonerate yourself under Rule 31.2 (one turn)

(b) protest another boat involved in the incident under Rule 60 (the other boat can accept a two-turns penalty or risk being disqualified later), or

(c) exonerate yourself by accepting a two-turns penalty if you think that besides touching the mark you also broke a rule yourself.

If you do nothing and continue sailing knowing that you hit a mark, you infringe the principle of 'Sportsmanship' and risk being disqualified under Rule 2 Fair Sailing. Contact with a mark by a boat's equipment constitutes touching it, see Case 77, but you do not necessarily break Rule 31 if you touch a mark that shifts as a result of another boat touching it. See Case 28.

✸*211*

✸*228*

31 Touching a Finishing Mark and Definition: Finishing

According to the definition of racing and Rule 31, if this boat touches the mark, even after she has crossed the finishing line, she must exonerate herself and does not finish until she crosses the line a second time. She must however be protested before she can be DSQ. See Case 128.

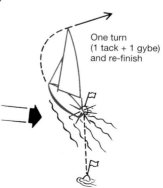

One turn
(1 tack + 1 gybe)
and re-finish

✸*211*

page

229✻

32   Shortening or Abandoning After the Start

When a race is abandoned after only a few boats finishing, their results stand and the Race Committee must consider redress to the boats that were still racing. See also Case 37 when abandoning races in a multi-class regatta.

PART 4 – OTHER REQUIREMENTS WHEN RACING

41   Outside Help

229✻

Except for Team Racing a boat is not allowed to receive outside help. There was a case where it was suspected that a crew was using a walkie-talkie radio to contact someone on shore. If it had been proved, then the boat would have been disqualified. When a boat is not in danger, advice that she seeks and receives that will help her to complete the race is outside help, even if it is sought and received on a public radio channel. See Cases 100 and 120.

41   Outside Help and
47.2 Limitations on Crew

If a boat loses a man overboard, she may receive help or assistance from another competitor or boat as long as no forward progress is made during the recovery operation.

42   Propulsion

229✻

World Sailing Interpretations of Rule 42 Propulsion were issued in April 2003 explaining to Sailors and 'on the water' Judges in detail how Rule 42 is interpreted and applied on the water. Latest revised version is available on the Sailing World website. See page 21.

229✻
230✻

Cases 5, 8 and 69 from the Casebook also contain interpretations of this rule and Case 132 explain when a boat is 'on a beat to windward'.

44.1 Taking a Penalty

If you hit a starting mark while racing, i.e. after the preparatory signal, you must complete your penalty as soon as possible (it might be before the starting signal except for a match race). If you hit a finishing mark you must complete your penalty before you can finish correctly by crossing the line again. See also Definitions: Racing and Finishing.

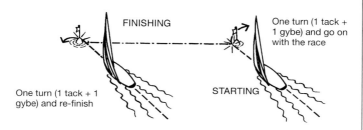

FINISHING

One turn (1 tack + 1 gybe) and go on with the race

One turn (1 tack + 1 gybe) and re-finish

STARTING

44.1 Taking a Penalty

When a boat retires as required by rule 44.1, whether out of choice or necessity, she cannot then be penalised further. See Cases 99 and 107.

*230/ 218

44.2 One Turn Penalty for Touching a Mark

After touching the mark, both these tracks will correct the error. The key to what has to be done is:

1 Sail clear of the other boats as soon as possible.
2 Promptly do one turn which must include one tack and one gybe; keep clear of other boats while turning.
3 Ensure the mark has been rounded correctly according to Rule 28.1.

See Case 108 for more examples

*230

One turn (1 tack + 1 gybe) and go on with the race

One turn (1 tack + 1 gybe) and go on with the race

45 Anchoring and Definition: Starting

A boat may anchor after her preparatory signal. Here Red has a part of her equipment on the wrong side of the line at the starting signal. However, Red has not started early since no part of her hull is over the line.

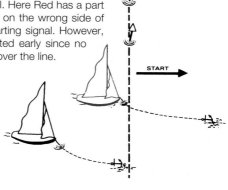

47.2 Limitations on Crew

When capsizing near the finishing line, a boat may finish with crew members in the water provided they have physical contact with the boat.

49.1 &
49.2 Crew Position

Crews racing in off-shore boats equipped with upper and lower lifelines of wire (not rope), are permitted to have their bodies outside the upper lifeline when sitting on the deck facing outboard. You must **sit** on the deck, not hike over the line and you may *not* use a 'device designed to position the body outboard'.

231 ❋   See Case 36 for illustrations of permitted and prohibited crew positions relative to lifelines.

231 ❋   Case 83 contains a further interpretation of this rule.

50 Competitor Clothing and Appendix H

In Appendix H2, a competitor whose weight of wet clothing and equipment exceeds the amount permitted may rearrange the clothing and equipment on the draining rack and repeat the test. This may be interpreted as reweighing the clothing and equipment piece by piece.

Drinking containers like 'camelbacks' must not be worn while racing. See Case 89.

✹*231*

51 Movable Ballast

Items of the boat's gear shall not be moved about the boat. Unless in use, gear must remain in its designated place.

55.3 Use of Outriggers

Be careful how you fix your jib fairleads so that they do not contravene this rule, but a hand holding out a sheet is not an outrigger, as it is not a 'fitting'. See Case 4.

✹*231*

The spinnaker sheet may be led over the main boom or through a block on the main boom. A guy is not a sheet so a jockey pole attached to a spinnaker guy is not an outrigger. See Case 97.

✹*231*

PART 5 – PROTESTS, HEARINGS, MISCONDUCT AND APPEALS

60 Right to Protest

The responsibility for protesting primarily rests with the competitors. The Race Committee is not burdened with knowing and enforcing the class rules when the members of the class themselves fail to do so. See Cases 39 and 68. Cases 1 and 80 also refer to the right to protest.

✹*232*
✹*232*

See also Case 141 for an interpretation of the word 'serious' when used in 'serious damage'.

✹*232*

61.1(a) Informing the Protestee, Protest flag

The flag must be flown at the first reasonable opportunity following an incident. See Case 72 for interpretation of the word flag. A protest is not lodged until it is written on paper and handed to the Race Committee. Do not be afraid to fly the protest flag if you are in any doubt. You may find when you get ashore that it is not necessary to continue with the protest, in which case you do not have to lodge it.

61.1(a) Informing the Protestee

A protesting boat must attempt to inform the protested boat but it is not mandatory that she succeeds in the attempt. But you must convince the Protest Committee of your attempts.

61.2 Contents

A protest shall be in writing. A boat that is involved in an infringement, but which she believes is not her fault, must nevertheless lodge a written protest if she wishes to clear herself. Citing the correct rule to have been broken is not necessary. See Case 22.

233

62 Redress

The Race Committee cannot be protested by a boat or a competitor. Instead the boat may seek redress only when she alleges that her finishing position has been significantly worsened by a fault made by the Race Committee and through no fault of her own. See Cases 44 and 142.

233

62.1(b) Redress

For interpretation of giving redress to a boat physically damaged from contact with a boat that broke a Part 2 rule see Case 110. 'Injury' refers to bodily injury for a person, and 'damage' is limited to physical damage to a boat or her equipment. For further interpretations of 'damage' and 'injury' see Cases 19, 110 and 135.

218/
233

233

For redress in a series see Case 116.

62.2 Redress

When a boat requests redress over an incident that she claims affected her finishing place in a race, and thus in a series, the time limit for making the request is the time limit for the race, rather than a time limit based on the posting of the series results. See Case 102.

233

page

63.2 Time and Place of Hearing

All information necessary for the competitors shall be available to them but they shall make an effort to obtain the information. See Case 48.

✹234

64.2 Penalties and Exoneration

Boat B on starboard was hit by boat C on port (1), and knocked on to the other tack. Boat B was now nearly stopped on port tack and was hit by boat D who was on starboard (2). Boat B is not wrong because she was compelled by C to break Rule 10. She should protest boat C, and be exonerated. In a protest arising from contact the Committee must find facts and give a decision on them. See also Cases 10 and 51.

234/
✹217

Separate protests in closely connected incidents should be heard together. See Case 49.

✹234

64.3 Decision on Redress

When a boat fails to finish correctly because of a race committee error, but no boats racing gain or lose as a result, an appropriate and fair form of redress is to score all the boats in the order they cross the line. See Case 45.

✹211

70 Right of Appeal

A boat may appeal only if she has been party to the protest. If she was not party to the protest, but was affected by the decision she must seek redress under the terms of Rule 62. See Case 55.

✹235

PART 6 – ENTRY AND QUALIFICATION

78   Certificates

With increasing regularity there are protests concerning these certificates. Owners must satisfy Rule 78.1 in making sure that their boat complies with the certificates issued to them. Provided this is satisfied then they cannot be retrospectively invalidated after a race or series is completed. See Case 57 for inter-pretation of Rule 78.

236✻

78   Certificates

236✻

Cases 130 and 131 decribes the role of measures, appointment, who can protest and who can DSQ.

PART 7 – RACE ORGANISATION

86   Rules Changes
89.2 Notice of Race
90.2 Sailing Instructions

Many clubs do not take enough trouble over the Notice of Race and Sailing Instructions. This often results in confusion, dis-appointment and bad feelings. It is really very simple for clubs to go through Rules 88.2, 89.2 and Appendices J, K and L and make out standard forms which can cover almost all races. Rule 86 specifies that the Sailing Instructions shall not alter some specified Rules. However other rules can be changed by referring specifically to the Rule and stating the change. If Rules are changed a strict procedure must be followed (Case 121). Note class rules may not alter a racing rule unless the alteration is permitted by the racing rule itself (Case 85). Committees should be careful not to say and change too much. It is highly recommended that the organisers use the Standard Sailing Instructions wherever possible, so that the competitors do not have to learn a whole new 'book' of Sailing Instructions for every event they go to. It should be a sailing contest not a reading contest.

236✻

237✻

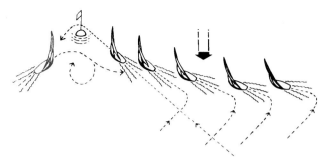

90.2 Sailing Instructions

The drawing illustrates some of the problems for Race Committees and shows the likely situation when the windward mark is rounded to port. The disadvantage of port rounding is that a boat approaching on port tack, even though she may really be leading as Red is here, may not be able to round the mark, and can drop many places. Also the tendency is to use only the starboard side of the course.

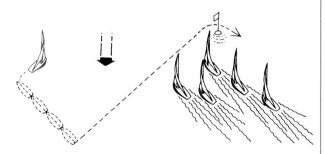

90.2   Sailing Instructions

With starboard rounding, a boat can always get round the mark by standing on a few lengths, but there are usually more protest situations.

90.2(c) Changes to Sailing Instructions

Unless there is a special procedure laid down in the Sailing Instructions, they cannot be changed unless by written amendment. Oral instructions can easily be misunderstood or even forgotten. See Case 32.

*237

APPENDIX C – MATCH RACING RULES

16   In match racing it is common for the right-of-way boat to alter course and 'hunt' the give-way boat while she is trying to keep clear. This is to gain a 'controlling' position, and she can do this without breaking Rule 16 as long as the give-way boat still has at least one opportunity to keep clear. A typical example is when the boats first meet after entering the starting area.

In the situation below, A luffs slowly to give way when there is still some distance between the boats. B responds by also luffing, maintaining a collision course 'hunting' A. A has no choice but to luff further and eventually to tack as the last possibility to keep clear. B now has a controlling position and can 'take' A to the left side of the course, the 'Red zone'. B will probably win the start.

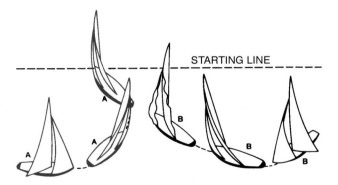

STARTING LINE

In the second situation D keeps bearing away until the boats are very close. Her only possibility to keep clear is then to luff hard. E can no longer 'hunt' because of Rule 16. She must let D pass to windward and cannot force her to tack. Instead the boats will probably go into a circling manoeuvre.

It is more risky for the port tack boat to meet on opposite tacks in the pre-start when the boats are closer to the wind because it is easier for the starboard tack boat to gain a controlling position.

STARTING LINE

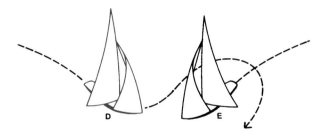

D   E

Umpired matches
When umpires are employed in match racing there will usually be one umpire boat with two umpires to each match. Each umpire will 'adopt' one boat. The umpire plays the role of 'his' boat and constantly states what she is doing, who is give-way boat and why. Thus the umpires 'discuss' the situation as it develops and often will have decided the infringement as it occurs. Let us follow the typical luffing situation in the pre-start manoeuvre shown overleaf.

A establishes an overlap from clear astern and luffs. A's umpire will follow if B was given room initially (Rule 15) and if A is luffing according to Rule 16. B's umpire will follow if B takes action to keep clear under Rule 11 and the definition of Keep Clear when A gets the overlap. The umpires also have to observe if the overlap is broken. When the collision occurs, the umpires have already in the left situation agreed that: (1) The overlap was not established too close and (2) A luffed slowly giving B room to keep clear (3) B did not take sufficient action to keep clear and establish a 'safety distance' from A and finally (4) B is through head to wind, ie she has tacked. All these circumstances put together amount to a penalty for B.

In the situation on the right, which is not very different and probably the way B saw the first situation, (1) D is establishing the overlap too close to E, not initially giving room for E to keep clear and (2) E has made a reasonable effort to try to keep clear. Penalty awarded to D.

It is obvious that there are other situations similar to these two where the decisions are not so clearcut. Competitors must remember that in match racing they do not have the opportunity to take their case to a jury. They must rely on the umpires' knowledge of the rules and their ability to follow the manoeuvres. In very complicated situations involving several rules, the umpires' view of the situation may be very different from that of the competitor. They should not risk a close situation when the decision can go either way. It is safer to try to 'give' the other boat a penalty in situations where the rights and obligations are more obvious and the worst you risk is a 'green flag'.

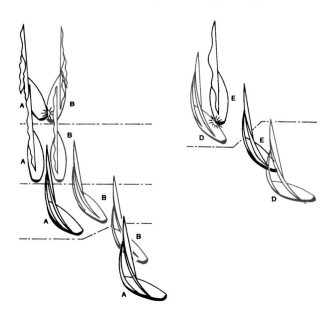

WORLD SAILING INTERPRETATIONS
OF THE RACING RULES (CASES)

Definitions

Finishing

Case 45. Two different races used the same mark as finishing mark. To avoid boats passing the finishing mark in opposite directions a sailing instruction changed the finish in one race to a 'hook round' finish. The sailing instructions cannot change a definition so the boats that finished according to the SI did not finish correctly. However since the race committee made an error in issuing an invalid sailing instruction, the boats that failed to finish correctly were entitled to redress. Since no boats gained or lost as a result of the error, the appropriate and fair form of redress for all boats was to score all the boats in the order they crossed the finishing line, without regard to the direction in which they crossed it.

Finishing

Case 82. When a finishing line is laid so closely in line with the last leg that it cannot be determined which is the correct way to cross it in order to finish in accordance with the definition, competitors are eligible for redress, and either direction is acceptable.

Finishing

Case 127. A boat clears the finishing line and marks when no part of her hull, crew or equipment is on the line, and no mark is influencing her choice of course.

Finishing

Case 128. Scores Determined by the Race Committee. If a boat makes an error under rule 28.2 or breaks rule 31 at the finishing line and finishes without correcting her error or taking a penalty, she must be scored points for the place in which she finished. She can only be penalized for breaking rule 28.2 or rule 31 if she is protested and the protest committee decides that she broke the rule.

Keep Clear

Case 77. Contact with a mark by a boat's equipment constitutes touching it. The fact that she touches because she has manoeuvring or sail-handling difficulties does not excuse her infringement. A boat obligated to keep clear does not break a rule when touched by a right-of-way boat's equipment that moves unexpectedly out of normal position. See however Case 91 below.

RULE NO

Keep Clear

Case 91. A boat required to keep clear of another boat's equipment out of its normal position when the equipment has been out of its normal position long enough for the equipment to have been seen and avoided. See Case 77 above.

Mark-Room

18.2
21

Case 144. An obligation to give mark-room continues until the entitled boat has passed the mark, leaving it on the required side. The definition Mark-Room defines the space a boat is required to give, and a boat is exonerated under rule 21 only if she is sailing within that space.

Obstruction

Case 41. W and L, who are over-lapped, are overtaking A, all on the same tack. A ranks as an obstruction to W and L and can be passed on either side. If L, the right of way boat, chooses to pass to leeward she must give room to W to pass inside. If L chooses to pass to windward, she is entitled to room, and W must keep clear. The inside boat is not required to hail for room, but it would be prudent to hail to avoid misunderstanding.

Proper Course

Case 14. Two boats on the same leg sailing near each other may have different Proper Courses. The faster of the two different courses cannot be determined in advance, and is not necessarily proven by one boat or another reaching the next mark ahead. When, owing to a difference of opinion as to proper course, two boats on the same tack converge, the windward boat must keep clear.

Proper Course

Case 46 refers to two boats on converging courses approaching the finishing line. In the absence of W, L would have luffed to finish at right angles to the line, but W wished to sail dead down wind to finish at the starboard end of the finishing line. L, establishing the overlap from clear astern, did not have the right to sail above proper course. However Rule 11 says that when two boats on the same tack overlap then the windward boat shall keep clear, even if L is limited by Rules 16 and 17.1. L's proper course was correct, and provided that she did not break Rule 16, she could sail up to her proper course.

Proper Course

Case 134. A boat's proper course at any moment depends on the existing conditions. Some of those conditions are the wind strength and direction, the pattern of gusts and lulls in the wind, the waves, the current, and the physical characteristics of the boat's hull and equipment, including the sails she is using.

Room

Case 103. Two 30-foot boats are overlapped on port approaching an obstruction. The boats are normally sailed by a crew of six but the inside boat is sailed by a relatively inexperienced crew of three. Neither the experience nor the number of crew is relevant in determining the 'room' needed to be given to the inside boat. The phrase 'seamanlike way' in the definition of room refers to the boat handling that can reasonably be expected from a competent, but not expert, crew of the appropriate number for the boat.

Room

11+
21(a)

Case 146. When boats are approaching a starting mark to start and a leeward boat luffs, the windward boat is exonerated under rule 21(a) if she breaks rule 11 while sailing within the room to which she is entitled under rule 16.1.

Rules

Case 98. The rules listed in the definition Rule apply to races governed by The Racing Rules of Sailing whether or not the NoR or SI explicitly state so. An SI, provided it is consistent with any prescription to Rule 88.2, may change some or all of the prescriptions of an NA. Generally neither the NoR nor SI may change a class rule. When a boat races under a handicapping or rating system, the rules of that system apply, and some or all of her class rules may apply as well. When the NoR conflicts with the SI, neither takes precedence.

Sportsmanship and the Rules

Case 65. A boat knows she has infringed the black flag rule, but continues to race in order to hinder a rival competitor. Under the principles of sportsmanship she is obliged to retire promptly. She is found to have committed a gross breach of good sportsmanship and therefore has broken Rule 2. She is excluded not only from that race, but from the series under Rule 69.1.

RULE NO
PART 1 – FUNDAMENTAL RULES

1.1   **Case 20**. Helping those in danger. Rendering assistance to those in danger is compulsory to those in a position to do so. It does not matter that help may not have been asked for, nor that subsequently it may be shown not to have been needed. So a boat rendering assistance may be entitled to redress.

2   **Case 47**. Fair Sailing. A boat that deliberately hails 'Starboard', when she is on port tack, has not acted fairly, and has broken Rule 2.

2   **Case 73**. W and L were overlapped. The crew of L deliberately touched W's deck with a hand and intimated that W should retire. W was disqualified but appealed successfully. When, by deliberate action, L's crew touches W, which action could have no other intention than to cause W to break Rule 11, then L breaks Rule 2.

2   **Case 74**. There is no rule that dictates how the helmsman or crew of a leeward boat must sit. Contact with a windward boat does not break Rule 2 unless either the helmsman's or crew's position is deliberately misused. In this case there was no indication of deliberate misuse from the leeward boat. See also Case 73 above.

2   **Case 78**. In a fleet race either for one-design boats or for boats racing under a handicap or rating system, a boat may use tactics that clearly interfere with or hinder another boat's progress in a race, provided that, if she is protested under rule 2 Fair Sailing, the protest committee finds that there was a reasonable chance of her tactics benefitting her final ranking in the event. However, she breaks rule 2, and possibly rule 69.1(a), if while using those tactics she intentionally breaks a rule.

5   **Case 66.** Protest committee. A race committee has no jurisdiction over a Jury and may not alter, or refuse to implement, the decision of a Jury or independent Protest Committee, including a decision based on a report from an authority qualified to resolve questions of measurement.

RULE NO
PART 2 – WHEN BOATS MEET

Preamble

Case 38. Sailing Instruction content. Between sunset and sunrise the International Regulations for Prevention of Collisions at Sea (IRPCAS) might replace the World Sailing rules. The IRPCAS are intended to ensure the safety of vessels at sea by precluding situations that might lead to collisions. They effectively prohibit a right-of-way boat from changing course (eg luffing) when she is close to a boat obligated to keep clear.

Preamble

Case 67. When a boat that is racing meets a vessel that is not racing, the Government right-of-way rules for the area concerned (usually the IRPCAS rules) apply. In this case the racing boat is the give-way boat, but deliberately rams the cruising boat. Not only has she infringed the preamble of Part 2 which obliges her to comply with the Government right-of-way rules but also she was penalised for gross misconduct under Rule 69.

Preamble

Case 109. The IRPCAS (upon the high seas and in waters connected therewith navigable by seagoing vessels) or Government right-of-way rules (other local rules for harbours, rivers, lakes and other inland waters) apply between a boat racing and a vessel that is not. However IRPCAS/Government rules only apply between boats that are racing if the sailing instructions say so, and in that case all of Part 2 rules are replaced. IRPCAS/government rules apply regarding safety, fog signals and lights according to Rule 48. An IRPCAS/Government rule may be made to apply by including it in the sailing instructions or in another document governing the event. A boat may protest another boat for a breach of IRPCAS/Government rules, but not if the incident is one which a boat sailing under Part 2 rules meets a vessel that is not.

Section A – Right of Way

10   **Case 50**. In a straightforward port and starboard case, a Protest Committee must inquire carefully into whether the starboard tack boat did actually bear away to avoid collision, and/or that there was genuine and reasonable apprehension of collision. If this was so, then the port tack boat should be disqualified. If not the protest should be dismissed.

10   **Case 23**. *Rule 10 Opposite tacks versus Rule 19 Passing Obstructions.* W and L were running on port tack. S overtakes first L and then W and sails between them. S has right-of-way under Rule 10 over both port tack boats; consequently W does not rank as an obstruction to S and Rule 19 does not apply between S and L.

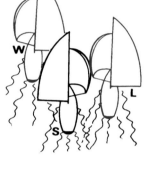

10   **Case 88**. S (starboard boat) and P (port boat) approached each other on a windward leg. When three lengths away, S hailed 'starboard' and again at two lengths. P did not respond. S, fearing collision luffed sharply and P bore away. Seeing this, S bore away also to swing her transom away and P passed astern of S within two feet. P was disqualified for not keeping clear. A boat may avoid contact and yet fail to keep clear.

10   **Case 43**. *Approaching a continuing obstruction on opposite tacks.* P was sailing close-hauled close to, and parallel with, a continuing obstruction. S approached on a collision course after completing a tack. As P had the time she should have kept clear of S after S tacked on to starboard and approached on a collision course.

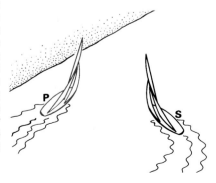

11   **Case 13.** *Same tack over-lapped before starting.* A boat does not break Rule 16 when holding a steady converging close-hauled course toward a windward boat even if she luffed before she came on converging course. Rule 11 applies; W must keep clear even if this means she is over the line early.

11   **Case 51.** This is a situation where there are intervening windward boats being prevented from luffing clear of a leeward boat and forced into breaking Rule 11 solely because of the most windward boat's failure to keep clear. The Protest Committee must exonerate boats when they are compelled by another to break a rule.

11   **Case 25.** *On the same tack and Rule 18.2(b) Mark-Room.* W and L were passing a leeward mark. L gave W necessary room to round but W was slow sheeting in after rounding the mark and so her boom hit L. Rule 18 ceased to apply when W had rounded and W had to keep clear under Rule 11. L could luff provided she did not break Rule 16. W was disqualified.

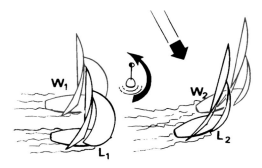

13   **Case 17.** *While tacking.* A boat has to keep clear under Rule 13 until she is heading on a close-hauled course, regardless of her movement through the water, or the sheeting of her sails.

Section B – General Limitations

14   ***Case 26***. *Avoiding Contact.* Two boats in different races were rounding the same mark in opposite directions. Rule 10 applied; P was disqualified. S claimed that had she changed course she would have broken Rule 16, but S was disqualified for failing to avoid a collision which resulted in damage. A right of way boat must act to avoid a collision when it is clear that the other boat is not keeping clear.

14   ***Case 107***. A boat that is not keeping a lookout may thereby fail to do everything reasonably possible to avoid contact. Hailing is one way that a boat may 'act to avoid contact'. When a boat retires she has taken a penalty and may not be penalised further for the same incident.

14   ***Case 87***. In a start, a starboard tack close-hauled boat S was struck amidships at right angles by a port tack boat. Realising the imminent collision, S altered course in the last moment but there was considerable damage. S was not disqualified under Rule 14. A right-of-way boat need not act to avoid contact until it is clear that the other boat is not keeping clear.

14   ***Case 123***. When it would be clear to a competent, but not necessarily expert, sailor at the helm of a starboard-tack boat that there is substantial risk of contact with a port-tack boat, the starboard-tack boat breaks rule 14 if contact occurs and there was still time for her to change course sufficiently to avoid the contact.

15   ***Case 27***. *Acquiring right of way.* A lee-ward boat L on port tack tacked on the starboard lay line and W had no time to avoid a collision. The Protest Committee disqualified L under Rule 15 but also disqualified W, pointing out that she knew that L was going to tack but did nothing to avoid collision. W appealed successfully. A boat is not required to anticipate that another boat will infringe a rule. A boat newly obligated by another boat's action is entitled to room to keep clear.

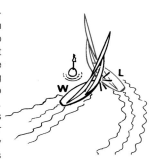

RULE NO

15   ***Case 24***. When A establishes a leeward overlap on B from clear astern, Rule 12 ceases to apply. B then becomes bound by Rule 11, A by Rule 15. The phrase 'room to keep clear' in Rule 15 means that A, in order to fulfil her obligation under Rule 11, must keep clear as best she can and, if this requires her to luff, she must do so. If this causes her to touch B, B has not given A enough room to keep clear. However, a clearly unnecessary or excessive luff by A causing contact with B infringes Rule 11. But B's obligation under Rule 15 is not a continuing one. If A fails to respond promptly after the overlap begins, B is no longer obligated.

15   ***Case 7***. *Overtaking to leeward.* When running towards a mark, L steered a course to overtake W and pass to leeward. The moment L established an overlap, W became subject to Rule 11. L at the same time became bound by Rule 15 and had to allow W room to keep clear. This obligation, however, is not continuative. L was also subject to Rule 17.1 and could not sail above her proper course. In this case, when approaching the mark, L luffed slightly and touched W. It was established that the luff was justified as being an alteration to a new proper course and W was therefore wrong under Rule 11.

15   ***Case 53***. Thirty seconds before a start W was dead in the water with sails flapping. L, approaching from leeward, hailed 'Leeward boat' before an overlap was established. L then had to bear away immediately when she established an overlap. W took no evasive action until after L had established an overlap. No contact was made. W, being clear ahead, need not anticipate her obligation to keep clear before being overlapped to leeward from clear astern. Neither boat was penalised as no rule was infringed.

15   ***Case 117***. When three boats are on the same tack and two of them are overlapped and overtaking the third from clear astern, if the leeward boat astern becomes overlapped with the boat ahead, the boat ahead is no longer an obstruction, and rule 19.2(b) does not apply. There are no situations in which a row of boats sailing close to one another is a continuing obstruction.

16   ***Case 6***. *Changing course.* When sailing to windward, P bore away to pass astern of S. S, however, tacked. P resumed her course after S had come on port tack close-hauled. There was no collision. In this case Rules 13 and 16 were complied with so no one was at fault. A starboard-tack boat that tacks after a port-tack boat has borne away to go astern of her is not necessarily breaking a rule.

RULE NO

16 ***Case 92***. S and P were approaching on a beat on opposite tacks in strong winds. When P bore away to keep clear S also bore away to 'hunt'. P bore away further but because of S heeling the rigs collided when the boats passed on opposite tacks. S was disqualified under Rules 16 and 14. When a right of way boat changes course the keep-clear boat is required to act only in response to what the right-of-way boat is doing at the time, not what she might subsequently do.

16 ***Case 52***. Rule 16 does not restrict the course of a keep-clear boat. In a typical match racing pre-start manoeuvre, one boat drives another away from the starting line. Boats A and B reached away from the starting line on port tack. A, moving faster, passed B and became clear ahead. As A luffed to tack so B luffed with her, preventing A from tacking. A then bore away to gybe but B bore away to leeward of her and prevented her from gybing. Rule 16 applies only to a right-of-way boat which B was not, either in position 3 or 4. In position 4, boat B clear astern had to keep clear under Rule 12 and A could not tack without infringing 13. At position 5, B was leeward boat and then held rights under Rule 11.

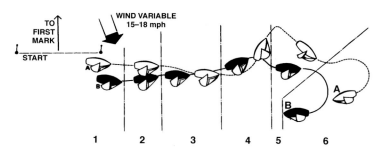

16 ***Case 60***. *Right-of-way boat changing course.* Port tack boat A rounded the windward mark to starboard and immediately gybed on to starboard. She decided, for tactical reasons, to reach high above it. As she luffed to her new course she came bow to bow with boat B on port tack still making for the mark. B bore away fast but it was not sufficient and A had to luff sharply as well to avoid a collision. There was no contact. A had no

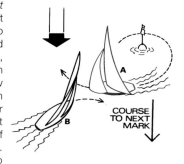

right to luff abruptly into the path of B for whatever reason. Tactical objectives do not relieve a boat of her obligations under the rules. A potentially serious situation occurred and only their combined efforts narrowly averted a collision. A was disqualified for infringing Rule 16.

16   *Case 76*. S and P are beating to the finishing line. S has overstood and sails free to round the Committee boat at the starboard end. P can cross S clear ahead until S luffs round the Committee boat when the boats are less than two lengths apart. Rule 18.2(a) does not apply (opposite tacks on a beat to windward). P must keep clear under Rule 10 but S's luff prevents her from keeping clear so S breaks Rule 16 even if she is sailing her proper course.

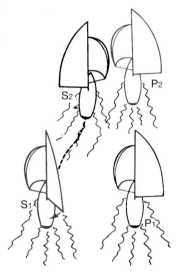

16   *Case 105*. After sailing alongside P for some time on port tack, S gybed to starboard without breaking Rule 15. Two minutes later S began to luff. P did not respond promptly and the boats touched. After S gybed Rule 15 only applied briefly and as right-of-way boat S was now only limited by Rule 16.1. When she luffed slowly she gave P room and P was required to react promptly, if necessary by gybing, to keep clear but she did not and therefore broke Rule 10 and Rule 14.

16
18   *Case 114*. Q&A 1. A, B and C are overlapped on the same tack reaching the zone of a mark, A outside C inside. A must give B mark-room including the space B needs to give C mark-room when B and C are both manoeuvring in a seamanlike way.

Room   Q&A 2. L, M and W are overlapped on the same tack L to leeward. L has no proper course restriction. If L luffs she must give room for M to keep clear including the space M needs to give room to W to keep clear.

Mark-
room   Q&A 3 + 4. L and W are overlapped on starboard approaching the starboard end startmark. L leaves room between her and the mark for W and W sails into the space that L freely gives. After W is committed between L and the mark L luffs. W luffs to keep clear

and hits the mark. L breaks rule 16 and W is exonerated for hitting the mark because L broke a rule. It does not matter if the starboard end mark is a mark or the committee boat. It is not seamanlike to luff somebody into a mark or an obstruction.

Section C – At Marks and Obstructions

18   **Case 70**. L and W were sailing on starboard tack overlapped approaching a windward starboard mark. W requested room and L replied ' Room will be given when needed'. One and a half lengths from the mark, the boats made contact: beam to beam. W was disqualified under Rule 11. A boat entitled to room under Rule 18 is relieved of her obligations under Rule 11 only to the extent that Rule 18 explicitly provides rights in conflict with Rule 11 and only when room as defined is being denied her. So W is not exonerated under Rule 21.

18.1(b)   **Case 9**. Two close-hauled boats meet at a starboard-hand windward mark. S has room to tack and round the mark but holds her course past the mark and forces P to tack. Rule 10 applies, not Rule 18 (opposite tacks on a beat to windward). There is no rule that requires a boat to sail a proper course.

18.2(a)   **Case 12**. *Overlap on widely differing courses.* OL, on starboard tack, approached a starboard-hand mark close-hauled. IW approached from almost directly upwind and called for room to round the mark inside OL. At the proper time IW had an overlap on OL under the definition and was therefore entitled to room under Rule 18.2(a).

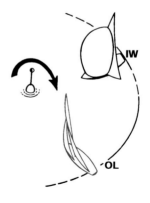

18   **Case 21**. *An interpretation of Room and Mark-Room.* 'Room' means enough space needed by an inside boat, which, in the existing conditions is handled in a seamanlike manner, to pass in safety between the object and the outside boat.

18   **Case 118**. In the definition Mark-Room, the phrase 'room to sail to the mark' means space to sail promptly in a seamanlike way to a position close to, and on the required side of, the mark.

RULE NO

18.2(a) **Case 59.** Four boats in line abreast are running towards a mark on starboard. A fifth boat B is just clear astern of the line of four. The two inside boats Al and A2 gybe on to port and round the mark satisfactorily. When A3 and A4 change course to gybe and round the mark, they are still outside the zone. This results in B becoming overlapped inside them before they enter the circle. They are able to give B room to round inside. By Rule 18.2(a) B is entitled to room to round the mark inside.

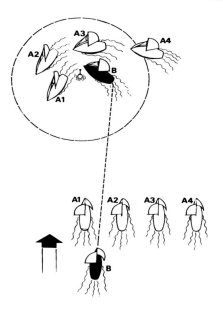

18.2(a) **Case 2.** *Not overlapped at mark.*
+(b) Boat O gybed from port to starboard when abreast of a starboard hand mark but outside the zone. The inside boat I was on port tack, but clear astern just before O's gybe, but was within the zone. When the boat clear astern reaches the zone first and they later become overlapped, 18.2(a) and not (b) applies and only as long as they remain overlapped and at least one of them is still in the zone. After B became clear ahead Rules 12 and 15 began to apply and O had to keep clear.

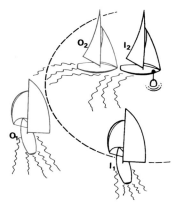

World Sailing Interpretations

18.2(c)   *Case 15*. Approaching a windward mark close-hauled, A is clear ahead but to leeward of B. A cannot tack if she thereby infringes Rule 13. B, however can prevent A from tacking but must keep clear if A luffs.

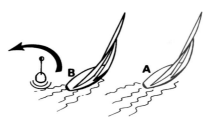

18.2   *Case 63*. At a mark, when room is made available to a boat that has no right to it, she may, at her own risk, take advantage of the room so given.

18.2(b)   *Case 81*. When two boats on the same tack are about to round **+ (c)**   a mark, Rule 18 applies even if they are on a beat. When one boat enters the zone clear ahead, Rule 18.2(b) applies. When the boat clear ahead then tacks, Rule 18.2(b) ceases to apply and she becomes subject to Rule 13 after passing head to wind and Rule 10 applies after she has reached close-hauled course.

18.2(b)   *Case 95*. Two boats are approaching a windward mark on port **+3(c)**   tack overlapped; W to windward just inside the zone, L one and a half lengths to leeward. L tacks for the layline without infringing Rules 13 or 15. W then tacks on top of L and luffs. L bears away to avoid W's transom and touches the mark. Rule 18 ceased to apply when L passed head to wind. When W also tacked Rule 18.3 began to apply and W was required to keep clear and give mark-room. W was disqualified under Rule 18.3. L was exonerated under Rule 64.

18.3   *Case 133*. Analysis of the application of rule 18.3 to a situation at a windward mark to be left to port in which two port-tack boats tack in quick succession to leeward of a starboard-tack boat that is fetching the mark. Both of the boats that tacked broke rule 18.3.

18.3(b)   *Case 93*. W completed a tack inside the zone directly ahead of L but with room for L to pass between W and the mark. L bore away, established an inside overlap and then luffed and touched W. Had L not luffed W would have kept clear. L was disqualified under Rules 15 and 16.

RULE NO

18.4 ***Case 75.*** Until an inside starboard-tack boat reaches the point in rounding a mark where her proper course is to gybe, an outside port-tack boat must keep clear under Rules 10 and 18.2. There is no conflict between Rules 10 and 18. Both apply and provide rights for the inside boat. But the inside boat is not to pass farther from the mark than necessary to sail her proper course (Rule 18.4) and if she luffs she must not break Rule 16.1.

19 ***Case 30.*** Two boats A and B are running on the same starboard tack alongside a continuing obstruction, A clear ahead of B. A is blanked by B and unintentionally gybes immediately followed by a collision. Because the boats are not overlapped neither Rule 19.2(b) nor 19.2(c) applied. B had to keep clear and broke Rule 12 and Rule 14 at the collision. A lost right of way by her unintended gybe but did not have room to keep clear.

19.2 ***Case 125.*** When an outside overlapped boat is required to give room to one or more inside boats to pass an obstruction, the space she gives must be sufficient to permit all the inside boats to comply with their obligations under the rules of Part 2.

19.2 ***Case 29.*** *Establishing an overlap at an obstruction.* W and L were running overlapped on the same gybe towards the finish, almost two lengths apart. M overtook and sailed between, establishing overlaps on both boats. There was no contact but W protested M for taking room she was not entitled to. L is an obstruction to W and M. M may sail between L and W provided that W is able to give room from the time the overlap begins. Protest dismissed.

19.2(b) ***Case 124.*** At any point in time while two boats are approaching an obstruction, the right-of-way boat at that moment may choose to pass the obstruction on either side provided that she can then comply with the applicable rules.

19.2(b) ***Case 11.*** W and L, overlapped, close-hauled on port tack approaches S, close-hauled on starboard tack. S is an obstruction. Normally W must tack if L calls. But in this case S was not an obstruction to L so L could not ask W to tack under rule 20.1. When L chooses to bear away to pass astern of S, W is entitled to room.

19, 20 ***Case 33.*** Two overlapping boats were close-hauled approaching a shore with projecting breakwaters. The leeward boat called for room to tack at the layline to the end of a breakwater but early for the shore. The windward boat must respond to the hail and her only remedy is to protest if she thinks the hail was early. After they both tacked the new inside boat was entitled to invoke Rule 18.2(a) to pass the outer end of a breakwater.

20.1   **Case 35**. *The amount of room required when tacking at an obstruction.* After a reply of 'You tack' to L's hail on approaching an obstruction, L completed a tack and bore away and was able to avoid W by three feet. L demonstrated by her actions that she had room to tack and clear W.

20.1   **Case 101**. A and B were approaching the shore close-hauled on starboard tack, A clear ahead and to leeward. A hailed for room to tack and B replied 'You tack'. A tacked and B held her course. After her tack, A was on collision course with B, but had room to keep clear by tacking to starboard. B therefore met her obligations under Rule 19.1.

20.1   **Case 54**. Two boats are approaching the shore on starboard tack. The leeward boat is a length ahead and a length-and-a-half to leeward. The leeward boat hails but is not heard. W does not respond but L tacks, tries to bear away underneath the stern of W but hits her several feet forward of the transom. On this instance it seems that the hail was not adequate and a second louder hail should have been made. L was disqualified under Rules 10 and 14. However normally the hailing boat's judgment of her own safety is conclusive.

20.1   **Case 113**. L, M and W are sailing close-hauled overlapped on starboard tack approaching the shore. L hails for room and it is clear that both M and W must tack and they can both hear the hail. M must respond to L's hail and therefore has to hail W for room. However W must also respond to L's hail and must not wait for M also to hail.

20.1(a)   **Case 3**. *Room to tack at an obstruction*. W and L, close-hauled and overlapped on port tack, were approached by S, close-hauled on starboard tack. S hailed for water; L hailed W to avoid S but obtained no response to three hails. S bore away to avoid a collision with L. W retired and S protested L who was disqualified under Rule 10. The Appeal Committee ruled that L did enough to satisfy her obligations. She was entitled to expect W to respond. She was not obliged to bear away astern of S or to anticipate W's failure to comply with Rule 20.1(a). So L was exonerated under Rule 64.1(a)

23.2   **Case 126**. For the purpose of determining whether rule 23.2 applies to an incident, a boat is sailing on the leg which is consistent with her course immediately before the incident and her reasons for sailing that course.

PART 3 – CONDUCT OF A RACE

26   **Case 31**. *Race signals at the start*. Under this rule the timing of starting signals is governed by the visual signal. There must also be a sound signal but it need not be made at the same moment. A boat is under an obligation to start correctly, but if she is unaware that she started incorrectly and the signals have been incorrect she may be granted redress.

28.1   **Case 90**. A and B started correctly but because of wind and current they drifted backwards, A outside the port end start mark and B back over the line. When the wind came back from a new direction they both passed outside the starboard end of the line and up the course. When their 'strings' are drawn taut A's will pass between the starting marks even if it makes an extra turn round the whole starting line, but B's string will not pass through the starting line. A complies with Rule 28 but B does not.

28.1   **Case 106**. When a boat's 'string' lies on the required side of the mark, it is not relevant that the mark also has been 'looped', for instance because a boat has been taken by the current.

28.1   **Case 129**. When the course is shortened at a rounding mark, the mark becomes a finishing mark. Rule 32.2(a) permits the race committee to position the vessel displaying flag S at either end of the finishing line. A boat must cross the line in accordance with the definition Finish, even if in so doing she leaves that mark on the side opposite the side on which she would have been required to leave it if the course had not been shortened.

28.2   **Case 58**. *Limit mark on the finishing line.* The inner limit mark was well on the post-finish side of the line. P crossed the line ahead of S, but well shorewards of the inner limit mark. Subsequently she passed the

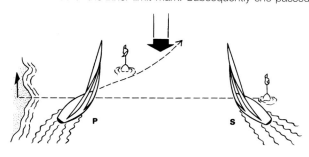

inner limit mark, leaving it to port. S, finishing after P, requested redress saying that the Race Officer had finished P before she had rounded the inner limit mark and therefore before she had completed the course. The request was refused. A buoy or other object on the post-finish side of the line is not a mark.

28.2 Sail the Course

Case 145. A boat's string, when drawn taut, is to lie in navigable water only.

29.1 + Race Signals

Case 71. Hailing sail numbers is not the sound signal required by Rule 29.1 when flag X is displayed. Boats failing to start correctly because they did not hear a hail of sail numbers may be granted redress if individual recall was not signalled with the required sound signal.

29.1   *Case 79.* Several boats were slightly over the middle of the line at their starting signal. The Race Committee did not signal 'individual recall' by flag X and sound signal until 40 seconds after the start. When a boat has no reason to know she is early and the 'individual recall' is not signalled promptly, this is an error by the Race Committee that entitles her to redress.

30.2   *Case 111.* If a boat is penalised under Rule 30.2 or 30.3 after a starting
30.3   sequence that results in a general recall, she can be penalised for that race even if the race in later starts is postponed before the starting sequence or during the sequence but before the starting signal.

30.3   *Case 96.* When, after a general recall, a boat learns from seeing her sail number displayed that she has been disqualified by the Race Committee and believes the Race Committee has made a mistake, her only option is not to start, and then to seek redress. However, if the race committee does not display her sail number and she sails in the restarted race, she should be scored BDF and not DNF.

31.3   *Case 28. Wrongfully compelled to touch a mark – abandoning after start.* A boat runs over a starting mark which sinks and re-surfaces, touching another boat on its pre-start side. Thus the second boat not only touched the mark but failed to start correctly since she passed the mark on the incorrect side. She has to return and re-start correctly to exonerate herself but she is not penalised for touching the mark. Abandonment is not an option open to the Committee in this case. Rule 32(d) abandoning after the start applies only to a mark that has shifted so that it is nowhere near its designated position.

32   ***Case 37**. Shortening or abandoning after the start*. Each race in a regatta is a separate race. In a multi-class regatta, abandonment may be suitable for some classes, but not for all.

PART 4 – OTHER REQUIREMENTS WHEN RACING

41   ***Case 100**. Three boats were about to round a mark near coastal rocks and sail into a 6-knot current. A radioed B whether it was safe to anchor in the vicinity of the mark. B answered it was not safe. A was protested by C and disqualified for receiving outside help because the answer was advice communicated to A in reply to a specific question, even if it was broadcast on a public frequency.

41   ***Case 120**. 'Information freely available' in rule 41(c) is information that is available without monetary cost and that may be easily obtained by all boats in a race. Rule 41(c) is a rule that may be changed for an event provided that the procedure established in the rules is followed.

42   ***Propulsion**. World Sailing has issued a special document 'Rule 42 Interpretations'. With that several other documents, booklets in different language, documents for judges, a Rule 42 Quiz and examples of common breaches in different classes. All to help sailors and judges to understand how rule 42 is interpreted and enforced on the water. Available on www.sailing.org/documents/ and www.sailing.org/raceofficials/rule42/index.php

42.1   ***Case 5**. Propulsion*. Recovering an anchor rapidly may be propulsion contrary to Rule 42.1. NB the case is withdrawn for revision.

42.1   ***Case 8**. Propulsion*. While reaching at good speed, a boat does not break Rule 42 when her helmsman, anticipating and taking advantage of following waves generated by a passing vessel, makes substantial helm movements timed to the passage of each wave. This is not sculling but using the natural action of water on the hull.

42.1   ***Case 69**. Propulsion*. Momentum of a boat after the preparatory signal that is the result of being propelled by her engine before the signal does not break Rule 42.1.

RULE NO

42.3(c)+ *Case 132. Interpretation 'on a beat to windward'.*

18.1(a) For the purpose of rule 18(a) Mark-Room:

1. when proper course for each of the boats is close-haulled or above, or

2. when one or both have overstood the close-hauled layline to the mark and are sailing below close-hauled.

For the purpose of rule 42.3(c) Propulsion

When her course to finish as fast as possibly in the absence of other boats is close-hauled or above.

43.1(c) *Case 19. Avoiding Contact, interpretation of 'damage'.* In considering whether damage occurred the following is suggested to be considered. Was the value of the boat, or part of the boat, diminished? Was anything made less functional?

44 *Case 99.* Mums 30s were racing in difficult conditions with winds of 20 knots. P broached and was out of control. From the moment it was apparent that P would not keep clear, the only action available to S, to try to avoid contact, was to crash gybe. S did not gybe and there was a collision causing considerable damage. S was disqualified under Rule 14 but this was reversed by appeal. This was because her only option was to crash gybe risking considerable damage and so it was not 'reasonably possible' to avoid contact and she did not break Rule 14, and could be entitled to redress. P retired under Rule 44.1. Whether it was out of choice or necessity, she could not be penalised further.

44 *Case 108.* When exonerating herself after touching a mark a boat needs to make a turn that includes a tack and a gybe, not necessarily a complete full 360° turn, and she may simultaneously be fulfilling the 'string rule' by rounding the mark provided she:

a) has sailed well clear of other boats,

b) is no longer touching the mark when beginning the turn,

c) is making the turn promptly after clearing other boats and

d) has not gained a significant advantage by touching the mark.

46 *Case 40. Person in charge.* Unless specifically stated in the Class Rules, Notice of Race or prescribed in the Sailing Instructions, the owner or person in charge of a boat is free to decide who steers her in a race, provided Rule 46 is not broken.

49.2   ***Case 83***. Repeated sail-trimming with the torso outside the lifelines is not permitted.

49.2   ***Case 36***. Positions 1, 2 and 3 do not break the rule; positions 5 and 6 break it. In position 4, on boats equipped with two wire lifelines, a crew member sitting on deck facing outboard with his waist inside the lower lifeline may have the upper part of his body outside the upper lifeline; otherwise the rule is broken.

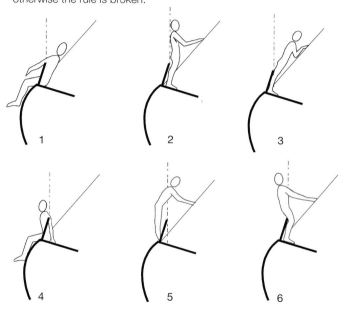

50.1(a)   ***Case 89.*** Wearing a drinking container on your person is not a necessity except on a sailboard. It is therefore considered to be for the purpose of increasing the competitor's weight and infringes rule 43.

55.3(a)   ***Case 4***. *Definition of an outrigger.* An outrigger is defined as a 'fitting', the crew's hand is not a 'fitting' and can therefore be used to hold a sheet outboard.

55.3   ***Case 97***. A spinnaker guy is not a sheet, so a jockey pole attached to a spinnaker guy is not an outrigger for a sheet.

RULE NO

PART 5 – PROTESTS, HEARINGS, MISCONDUCT AND APPEALS

Section A – Protests

60 *Case 39*. After a series several boats protested A for breaking a class rule limiting the crew to two. The protests were refused because none of the protesting boats had displayed protest flags. This decision was appealed on the grounds that the Race Committee ought, on its own initiative, to have protested A in all the races. Appeal dismissed. A Race Committee is under no obligation to protest a boat.

60 *Case 80*. When A crossed the finishing line she was scored DNF because the Race Committee believed she had failed to sail the course correctly. A requested redress claiming she had finished according to the definition. Redress was denied but A appealed and was reinstated. Without a hearing, a boat may not be penalised for failing to sail the course. A protest hearing and decision must be limited to a particular incident that has been described in the protest so A could not be penalised for failing to sail the course during the redress hearing. The Race Committee should have protested A for failing to sail the course.

60.1 *Case 1*. *Right to protest.* A boat which breaks a rule during a race and continues, can subsequently protest over a later incident even though she is disqualified after the race for the first incident.

60.1 *Case 68*. *Right to protest – sportsmanship.* The principles of sportsmanship obligate a boat to take a penalty or retire when she realises that she has broken a rule, but if she continues to race she retains her rights under Part 2 and her right to protest or request redress. The failure of a Race Committee to discover that a rating certificate is invalid does not entitle another boat to redress.

60.3(a) *Case 141.* *Interpretation of the term 'serious damage'.* It may include;
1   reduced safety of the crew?
2   significant adverse impacts of the boat's sailing performance?
3   significant cost of repair relative to value of boat?
4   significant reduction of boat value after repair?

61.1(a) *Case 72*. An object used as a flag must visually communicate the message 'I intend to protest' with little or no possibility of causing confusion on the part of the other competitors. A flag must be seen primarily to be a flag.

RULE NO

61.1(a)   *Case 112*. If one boat makes an error in sailing the course, a second boat may notify the first that she intends to protest when the error is made, or at the first reasonable opportunity after the first boat finishes, or any time in-between.

61.2(c)   *Case 22*. A Protest Committee's refusal of a protest cannot be justified by the fact that the rule alleged to have been infringed and cited in the protest was incorrect.

62   *Case 44*. *Redress.* A boat may request redress under the provisions of Rule 62, but only on the grounds that, through no fault of her own, an improper act or omission of the Race Committee made her finishing position significantly worse. The rules do not permit a Race Committee to be protested or penalised.

62   *Case 102*. S requested redress at the end of an 8-race series over an incident in Race 5 three weeks earlier. The protest was not valid. The effect of the incident on her result in the series was only through its effect on her finishing place in Race 5, so the relevant time limit for requesting redress was the time limit for Race 5.

62.1(b)   *Case 110*. A boat physically damaged from contact with a boat that was breaking a rule of Part 2 is eligible for redress only if the damage itself significantly worsened her score. Contact is not necessary for one boat to cause injury or physical damage to another. A worsening of a boat's score caused by an avoiding manoeuvre is not, by itself, grounds for redress, but damage or injury caused by the manoeuvre could be. 'Injury' refers to bodily injury to a person, and 'damage' is limited to physical damage to a boat or her equipment.

62.1(b)   *Case 116*. A discussion of redress in a situation in which a boat is damaged early in a series, is entitled to redress under rule 62.1(b), and is prevented by the damage from sailing the remaining races. In such a situation to be fair to the other boats in the series, the protest committee should ensure that fewer than half of the race scores included in her series are based on average points.

62.1(b)   *Case 135*. If a boat breaks a rule of Part 2 by failing to keep clear, the right-of way boat, or a third boat, may be entitled to redress if she is physically damaged, even if the damage is not caused directly by a collision with the boat that was required to keep clear.

62.1(b)   *Case 142.* When a boat requests redress because of injury or physical damage caused by the action of a boat breaking a Part 2 rule, she need not protest the boat that caused the injury/damage but her request will not succeed unless the protest committee conclude that the other boat broke a Part 2 rule.

Section B – Hearings and Decisions

63.2   ***Case 48***. A helmsman appealed a decision on the grounds that he was aware that a hearing was being held only when he was told to attend it. He had to read the protest while the hearing was in progress, and was not given time to prepare. The protest had been lodged in time, the time of the hearing had been posted correctly and the protest had been available for reading for more than an hour. Part 5 aims to protect a boat from miscarriage of justice, not to provide loopholes for protestees. A protestee has a duty to protect himself by acting reasonably before a hearing.

64.2   ***Case 10***. P on port did not keep clear and caused M on starboard to tack and make contact with S. P retired but M was disqualified. M appealed successfully. When two boats make contact, both may be exonerated when the situation was caused by a third boat that infringed a rule.

64.2   ***Case 49***. Two boats, PL and PW, were broad reaching in a lot of wind on port tack. They were on a collision course with boat S which was beating to windward on starboard tack. S was an obstruction to PW under Rule 19.2(b) who required room from PL to avoid a collision. There was contact of rigging between S and PW. S protested PW and PW protested PL. The protests were heard separately. PW was disqualified under Rule 10 and PL under Rule 19.2(b). PW appealed and was reinstated. Rule 10 required the port tack boat to keep clear but PW was unable to, because PL did not give sufficient room. No hail was required by PW as both port gybe boats were aware of boat S. When protests arise from the same, or closely connected incidents, it is advisable to hear them together in the presence of all the boats involved.

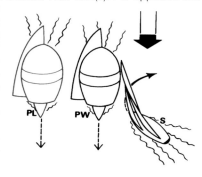

RULE NO
66   ***Case 115***. In rule 66 evidence is 'new' if, before or at the time of the original hearing; it was not reasonably possible for the party asking for the reopening to have discovered it, the protest committee is satisfied it was diligently but unsuccessfully sought by the party asking for the reopening or, the protest committee learns from any source that it not available to the parties.

Section C – Gross Misconduct

69.1   ***Case 34***. *Action by a Protest Committee and Rule 2, Fair Sailing.* Deliberately starting prematurely and harassing another boat in order to win a series constitutes gross infringement of the rules and sportsmanship, and could be the basis for action by the Protest Committee under Rule 69.1. Exclusion from the entire series would have been well within the spirit of the Racing Rules.

69.2(c) ***Case 122***. An interpretation of the legal term 'comfortable satisfaction', one of three 'standards of proof' relevant for jury members in Rule 69 hearings.

Section D – Appeals

70   ***Case 55***. *Right of appeal.* A 'protested' the Race Committee because of inadequate rescue facilities in contravention of the club's deeds. The Race Committee abandoned the completed race. B's appeal was denied. A boat has no right of appeal from a redress decision when she is not involved in the hearing. When she believes that her finishing position has been made worse by the decision she must herself request redress. She may then appeal the decision of that hearing.

71.4   ***Case 61***. *Appeal decisions.* When the decision of a Protest Committee is reversed upon appeal, the final standings and the awards must be adjusted accordingly.

PART 6 – ENTRY AND QUALIFICATION

78   **Case 130**. A person appointed to serve as an equipment inspector or event measurer is a member of the race committee only if appointed by that committee. Such a person must always make a report when one is required by rule 43.1(c) or rule 78.3. He may protest a boat under rule 60.2's last sentence only if the race committee delegates the responsibility for such protests to him.

78   **Case 131**. When a boat breaks rule 78.2, the race committee cannot disqualify her without a protest.

78.3   **Case 57**. *Compliance with class rules.* Two IOR-rated boats sailed in a summer-long series. A was later found to have sailed the series with an incorrect rating certificate. B requested redress. It was subsequently found by the National Rating Authority that there was an error in the rating certificate dating from the first hull measurement some years back. The Protest Committee found that the owner of boat A was not responsible for the error and that he had not infringed Rule 78.1. The Protest Committee decided that the Race Committee was not responsible for the error and therefore boat B was not entitled to redress. An in-date, duly authenticated certificate, presented in good faith, by an owner who has complied with the requirements of Rule 78.1, cannot be retrospectively invalidated after a race or series is completed.

PART 7 – RACE ORGANISATION

86   **Case 121**. This three-step procedure must be followed to change a racing rule for an event.
        1   Determine using Rule 86 whether or not the rule you wish to change may be changed. If yes
        2   Publish a notice of race (rule 89.2) and if the change in the rule would help competitors decide whether to attend the event or would provide them with information they will need before the sailing identify the rule that will be changed and include a summary of the change. Note: an addition to a rule or deletion of all or part of it is a 'change' to the rule.
        3   Publish written sailing instructions (rule 90.2(a)). Rule J2.2(3) requires the race committee to include in the sailing instructions an instruction that specifically identifies the rule that is changed and states the change.

RULE NO

86.1c   ***Case 85***. A class tried to delete Rule 61.1 which requires flying of protest flag. Rule 61 is not listed in Rule 86.1(c) among rules that the class rules can change. Class rules may not alter a racing rule unless the alteration is permitted by the racing rule itself.

89.1   ***Case 143.*** When the organisation authority for a race is not an organisation specified in rule 89.1, a party to a hearing does not have access to the appeal process, so take care what races you enter.

89.2c   ***Case 32***. *Change in sailing instructions and oral briefing.* The sailing instructions cannot require a competitor to attend an oral briefing. He is entitled to expect all necessary information to be contained in the written sailing instructions, possibly with amendments made in accordance with Rule 86.2.

App A3 ***Case 119***. When a race is conducted for boats racing under a rating system, the rating that should be used to calculate a boat's corrected time is her rating at the time the race is sailed. Her score should not be changed if later the rating authority, acting on its own volition, changes her rating.

App P5 ***Case 104***. Attempting to distinguish between facts and conclusions in a protest committee's findings is sometimes unsatisfactory because findings may be based partially on fact and partially on a conclusion. A national authority can change a protest committee's decision and any other findings that involve reasoning or judgement, but not one of fact. A national authority may derive additional facts by logical deduction. Neither written facts nor facts by diagram take precedence over the other. Protest committees must resolve conflicts between facts when so required by a national authority.

RACE SIGNALS

The meanings of visual and sound signals are stated below. For the colour of flags and sound signals see back cover. When a visual signal is displayed over a class flag, the signal applies only to that class.

AP Races not started are **postponed**. The warning signal will be made 1 minute after removal unless at that time the race is *postponed* again or *abandoned*.

AP over a numeral pennant 1–9: *Postponement* of 1–9 hours from the scheduled starting time.

AP over H: Races not started are *postponed*. Further signals ashore.

AP over A: Races not started are *postponed*. No more racing today.

C The position of the next *mark* has been changed.

I Rule 30.1 is in effect.

L Ashore: A notice to competitors has been posted.
Afloat: Come within hail or follow this boat.

M The object displaying this signal replaces a missing *mark*.

N All races that have started are **abandoned**. Return to the starting area. The warning signal will be made 1 minute after removal unless at that time the race is *abandoned* again or *postponed*.

N over H: All races are **abandoned**. Further signals ashore.

N over A: All races are **abandoned**. No more racing today.

P Preparatory signal.

S The course has been shortened.
Rule 32.2 is in effect.

U Rule 30.3 is in effect.

V Monitor communication channel for safety instructions (see rule 37).

X Individual recall.

Y Wear a personal flotation device.

Z Rule 30.2 is in effect.

First substitute: General recall. The warning signal will be made 1 minute after removal.

Black flag: Rule 30.4 is in effect.

Orange flag: The staff displaying this flag is one end of the starting line.

Blue flag: The staff displaying this flag is one end of the finishing line.